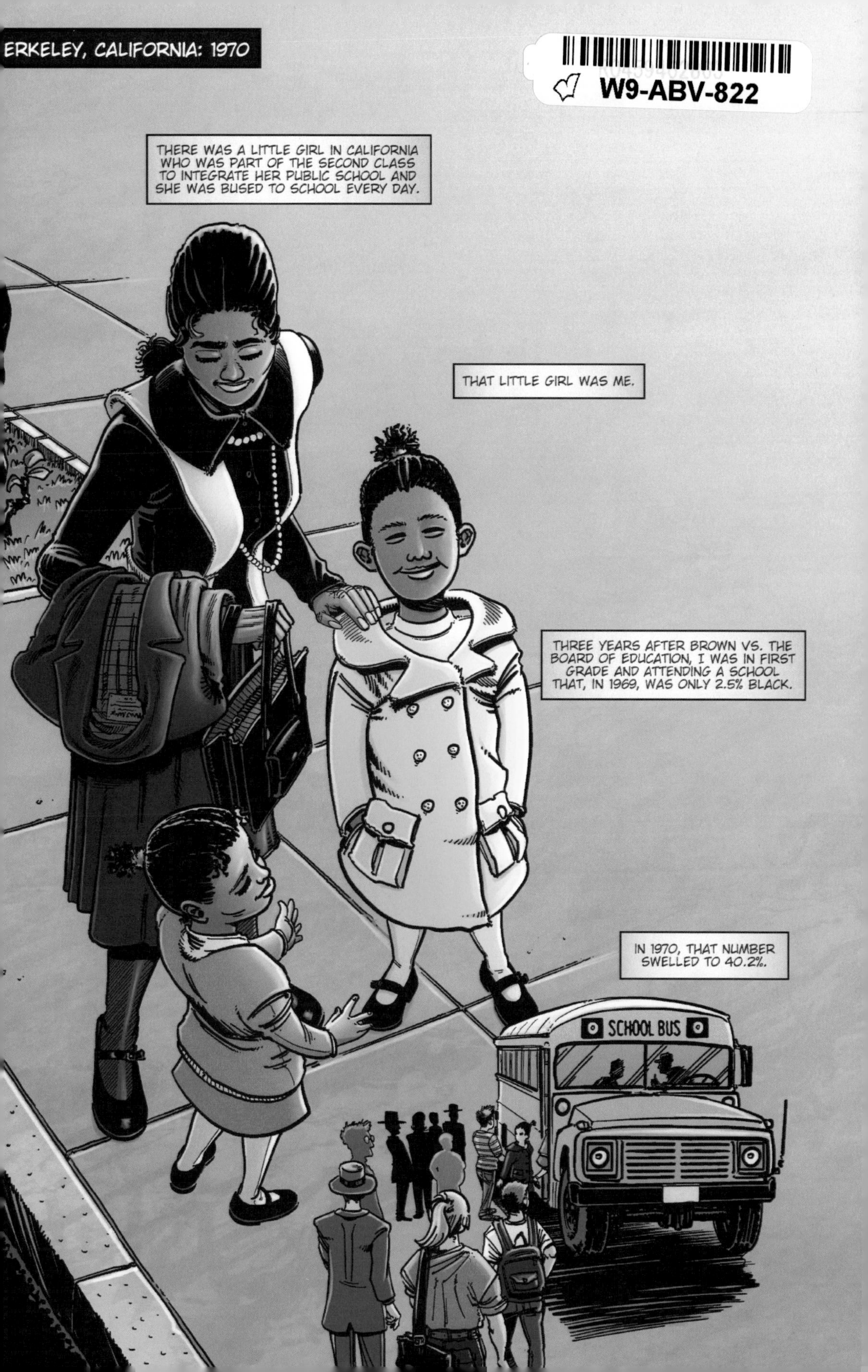
ERKELEY, CALIFORNIA: 1970
THERE WAS A LITTLE GIRL IN CALIFORNIA WHO WAS PART OF THE SECOND CLASS TO INTEGRATE HER PUBLIC SCHOOL AND SHE WAS BUSED TO SCHOOL EVERY DAY.
THAT LITTLE GIRL WAS ME.
THREE YEARS AFTER BROWN VS. THE BOARD OF EDUCATION, I WAS IN FIRST GRADE AND ATTENDING A SCHOOL THAT, IN 1969, WAS ONLY 2.5% BLACK.
IN 1970, THAT NUMBER SWELLED TO 40.2%.
SCHOOL BUS

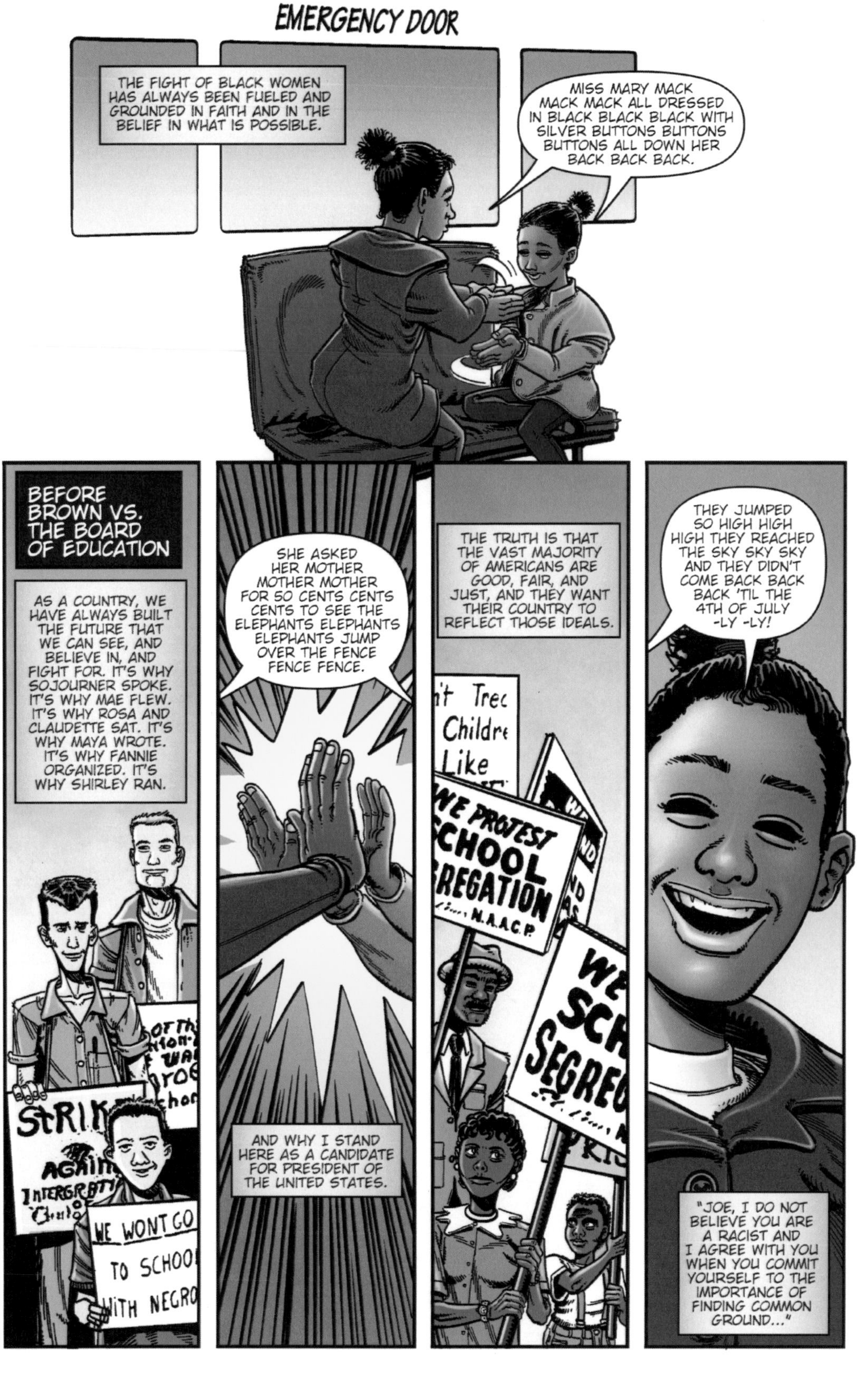
EMERGENCY DOOR
THE FIGHT OF BLACK WOMEN HAS ALWAYS BEEN FUELED AND GROUNDED IN FAITH AND IN THE BELIEF IN WHAT IS POSSIBLE.
MISS MARY MACK MACK MACK ALL DRESSED IN BLACK BLACK BLACK WITH SILVER BUTTONS BUTTONS BUTTONS ALL DOWN HER BACK BACK BACK.
BEFORE BROWN VS. THE BOARD OF EDUCATION
AS A COUNTRY, WE HAVE ALWAYS BUILT THE FUTURE THAT WE CAN SEE, AND BELIEVE IN, AND FIGHT FOR. IT'S WHY SOJOURNER SPOKE. IT'S WHY MAE FLEW. IT'S WHY ROSA AND CLAUDETTE SAT. IT'S WHY MAYA WROTE. IT'S WHY FANNIE ORGANIZED. IT'S WHY SHIRLEY RAN.
StRIK
WE WONT GO TO SCHOO WITH NEGRO
SHE ASKED HER MOTHER MOTHER MOTHER FOR 50 CENTS CENTS CENTS TO SEE THE ELEPHANTS ELEPHANTS ELEPHANTS JUMP OVER THE FENCE FENCE FENCE.
AND WHY I STAND HERE AS A CANDIDATE FOR PRESIDENT OF THE UNITED STATES.
THE TRUTH IS THAT THE VAST MAJORITY OF AMERICANS ARE GOOD, FAIR, AND JUST, AND THEY WANT THEIR COUNTRY TO REFLECT THOSE IDEALS.
Childre Like
WE PROTEST SCHOOL SEGREGATION N.A.A.C.P.
THEY JUMPED SO HIGH HIGH HIGH THEY REACHED THE SKY SKY SKY AND THEY DIDN'T COME BACK BACK BACK 'TIL THE 4TH OF JULY -LY -LY!
"JOE, I DO NOT BELIEVE YOU ARE A RACIST AND I AGREE WITH YOU WHEN YOU COMMIT YOURSELF TO THE IMPORTANCE OF FINDING COMMON GROUND..."

BUT THAT IS NOT OUR STORY.

...BUT I ALSO BELIEVE – AND IT'S PERSONAL – IT WAS ACTUALLY HURTFUL TO HEAR YOU TALK ABOUT THE REPUTATIONS OF TWO UNITED STATES SENATORS WHO BUILT THEIR REPUTATIONS AND CAREERS ON THE SEGREGATION OF RACE IN THIS COUNTRY.

SO I WILL TELL YOU. ON THIS SUBJECT – THE SUBJECT OF RACE – IT CANNOT BE AN INTELLECTUAL DEBATE AMONG DEMOCRATS.

WE HAVE TO TAKE IT SERIOUSLY.

FIRST DEMOCRATIC DEBATE, MIAMI, FL: JUNE 29, 2019

THAT IS NOT WHO WE ARE. THAT IS NOT OUR AMERICA.

AMERICA IS A COLLECTION OF IDEAS AND BELIEFS. WHEN IT WORKS, IT'S A BEAUTIFUL THING. BUT IT HAS TO WORK FOR ALL OF

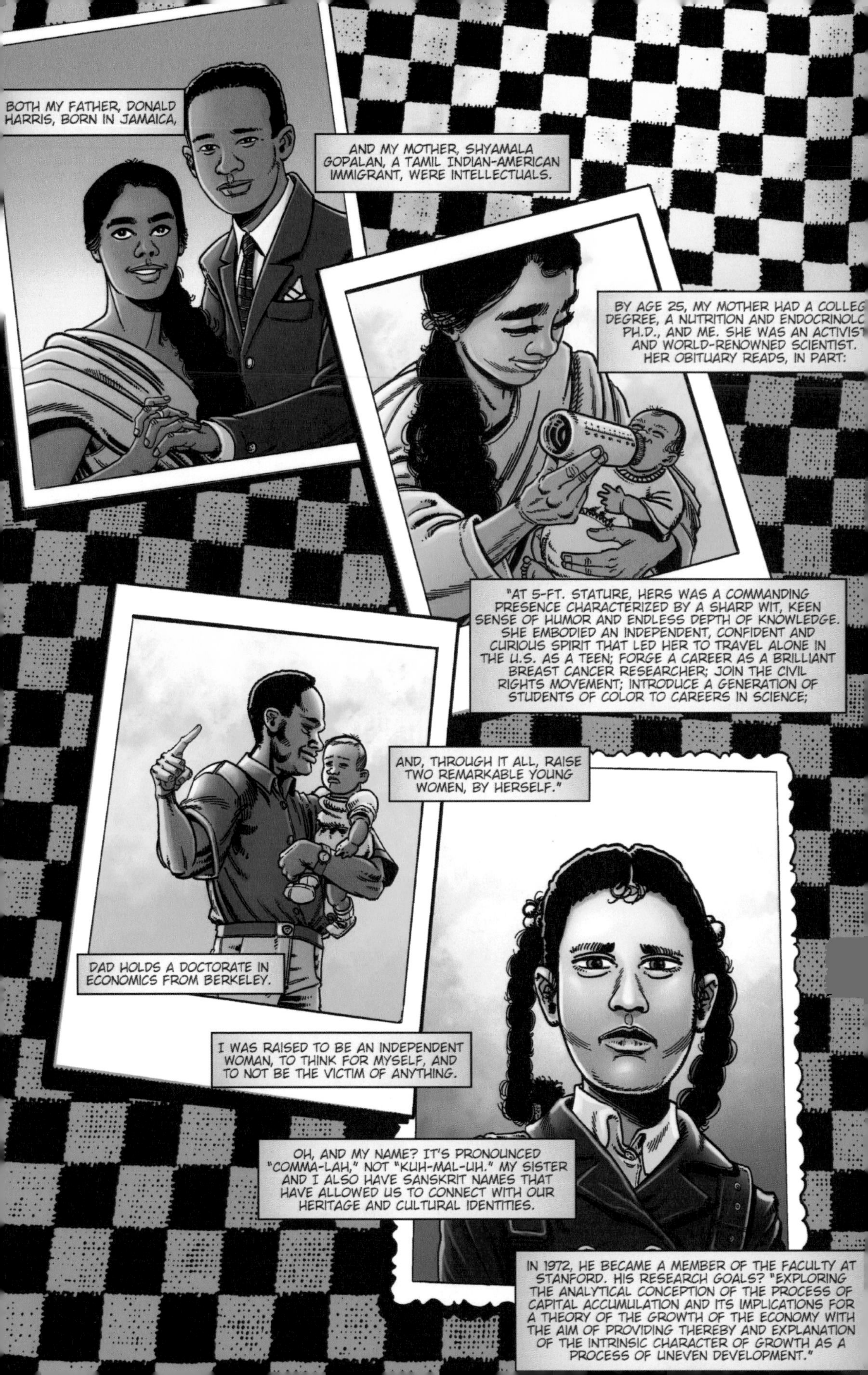
BOTH MY FATHER, DONALD HARRIS, BORN IN JAMAICA,
AND MY MOTHER, SHYAMALA GOPALAN, A TAMIL INDIAN-AMERICAN IMMIGRANT, WERE INTELLECTUALS.
BY AGE 25, MY MOTHER HAD A COLLEG DEGREE, A NUTRITION AND ENDOCRINOLO PH.D., AND ME. SHE WAS AN ACTIVIST AND WORLD-RENOWNED SCIENTIST. HER OBITUARY READS, IN PART:
"AT 5-FT. STATURE, HERS WAS A COMMANDING PRESENCE CHARACTERIZED BY A SHARP WIT, KEEN SENSE OF HUMOR AND ENDLESS DEPTH OF KNOWLEDGE. SHE EMBODIED AN INDEPENDENT, CONFIDENT AND CURIOUS SPIRIT THAT LED HER TO TRAVEL ALONE IN THE U.S. AS A TEEN; FORGE A CAREER AS A BRILLIANT BREAST CANCER RESEARCHER; JOIN THE CIVIL RIGHTS MOVEMENT; INTRODUCE A GENERATION OF STUDENTS OF COLOR TO CAREERS IN SCIENCE;
AND, THROUGH IT ALL, RAISE TWO REMARKABLE YOUNG WOMEN, BY HERSELF."
DAD HOLDS A DOCTORATE IN ECONOMICS FROM BERKELEY.
I WAS RAISED TO BE AN INDEPENDENT WOMAN, TO THINK FOR MYSELF, AND TO NOT BE THE VICTIM OF ANYTHING.
OH, AND MY NAME? IT'S PRONOUNCED "COMMA-LAH," NOT "KUH-MAL-UH." MY SISTER AND I ALSO HAVE SANSKRIT NAMES THAT HAVE ALLOWED US TO CONNECT WITH OUR HERITAGE AND CULTURAL IDENTITIES.
IN 1972, HE BECAME A MEMBER OF THE FACULTY AT STANFORD. HIS RESEARCH GOALS? "EXPLORING THE ANALYTICAL CONCEPTION OF THE PROCESS OF CAPITAL ACCUMULATION AND ITS IMPLICATIONS FOR A THEORY OF THE GROWTH OF THE ECONOMY WITH THE AIM OF PROVIDING THEREBY AND EXPLANATION OF THE INTRINSIC CHARACTER OF GROWTH AS A PROCESS OF UNEVEN DEVELOPMENT."

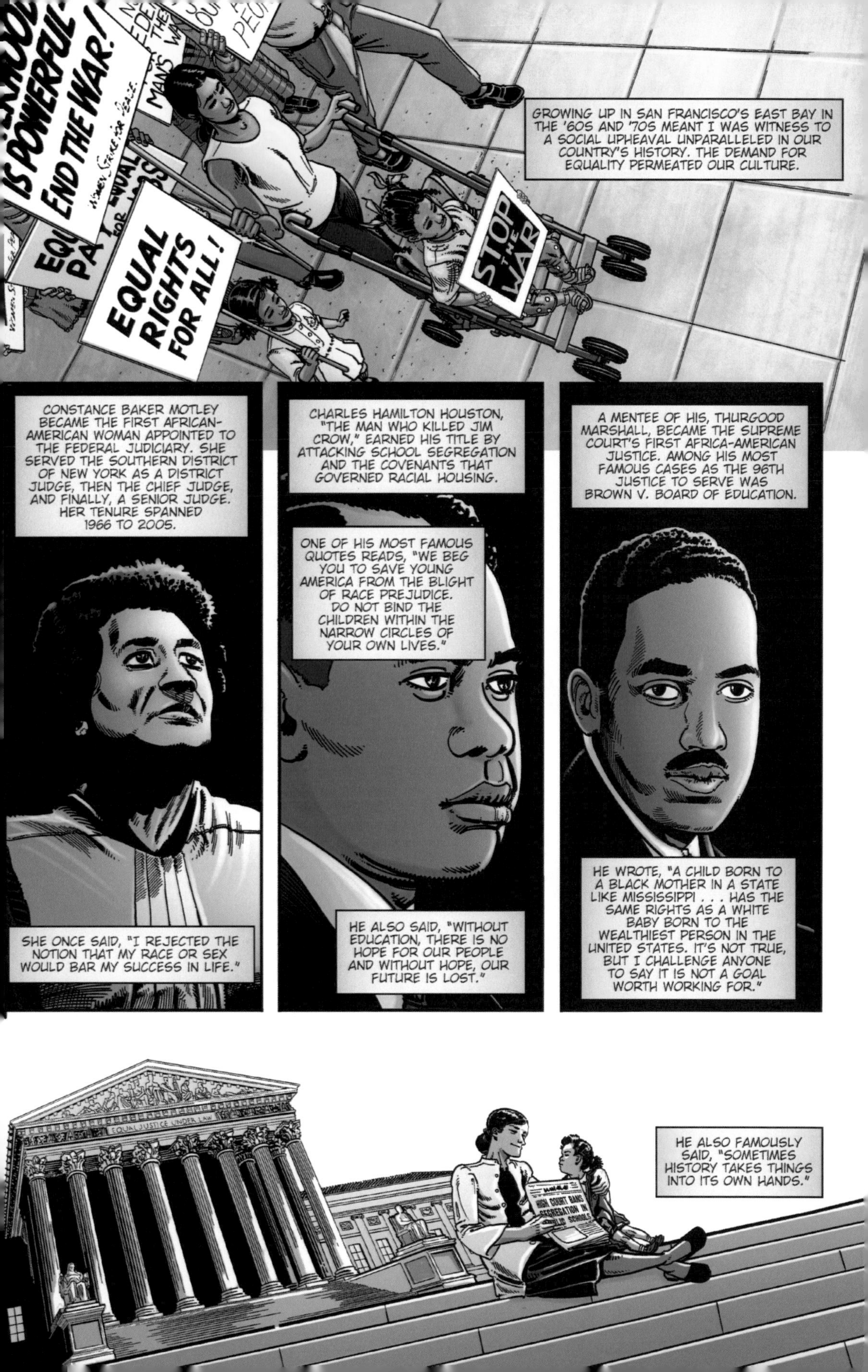

IS POWERFUL
END THE WAR!
WOMEN STRIKE FOR PEACE
EQUAL RIGHTS FOR ALL!
STOP THE WAR
GROWING UP IN SAN FRANCISCO'S EAST BAY IN THE '60S AND '70S MEANT I WAS WITNESS TO A SOCIAL UPHEAVAL UNPARALLELED IN OUR COUNTRY'S HISTORY. THE DEMAND FOR EQUALITY PERMEATED OUR CULTURE.
CONSTANCE BAKER MOTLEY BECAME THE FIRST AFRICAN-AMERICAN WOMAN APPOINTED TO THE FEDERAL JUDICIARY. SHE SERVED THE SOUTHERN DISTRICT OF NEW YORK AS A DISTRICT JUDGE, THEN THE CHIEF JUDGE, AND FINALLY, A SENIOR JUDGE. HER TENURE SPANNED 1966 TO 2005.
SHE ONCE SAID, "I REJECTED THE NOTION THAT MY RACE OR SEX WOULD BAR MY SUCCESS IN LIFE."
CHARLES HAMILTON HOUSTON, "THE MAN WHO KILLED JIM CROW," EARNED HIS TITLE BY ATTACKING SCHOOL SEGREGATION AND THE COVENANTS THAT GOVERNED RACIAL HOUSING.
ONE OF HIS MOST FAMOUS QUOTES READS, "WE BEG YOU TO SAVE YOUNG AMERICA FROM THE BLIGHT OF RACE PREJUDICE. DO NOT BIND THE CHILDREN WITHIN THE NARROW CIRCLES OF YOUR OWN LIVES."
HE ALSO SAID, "WITHOUT EDUCATION, THERE IS NO HOPE FOR OUR PEOPLE AND WITHOUT HOPE, OUR FUTURE IS LOST."
A MENTEE OF HIS, THURGOOD MARSHALL, BECAME THE SUPREME COURT'S FIRST AFRICA-AMERICAN JUSTICE. AMONG HIS MOST FAMOUS CASES AS THE 96TH JUSTICE TO SERVE WAS BROWN V. BOARD OF EDUCATION.
HE WROTE, "A CHILD BORN TO A BLACK MOTHER IN A STATE LIKE MISSISSIPPI . . . HAS THE SAME RIGHTS AS A WHITE BABY BORN TO THE WEALTHIEST PERSON IN THE UNITED STATES. IT'S NOT TRUE, BUT I CHALLENGE ANYONE TO SAY IT IS NOT A GOAL WORTH WORKING FOR."
EQUAL JUSTICE UNDER LAW
HIGH COURT BANS SEGREGATION IN PUBLIC SCHOOLS
HE ALSO FAMOUSLY SAID, "SOMETIMES HISTORY TAKES THINGS INTO ITS OWN HANDS."

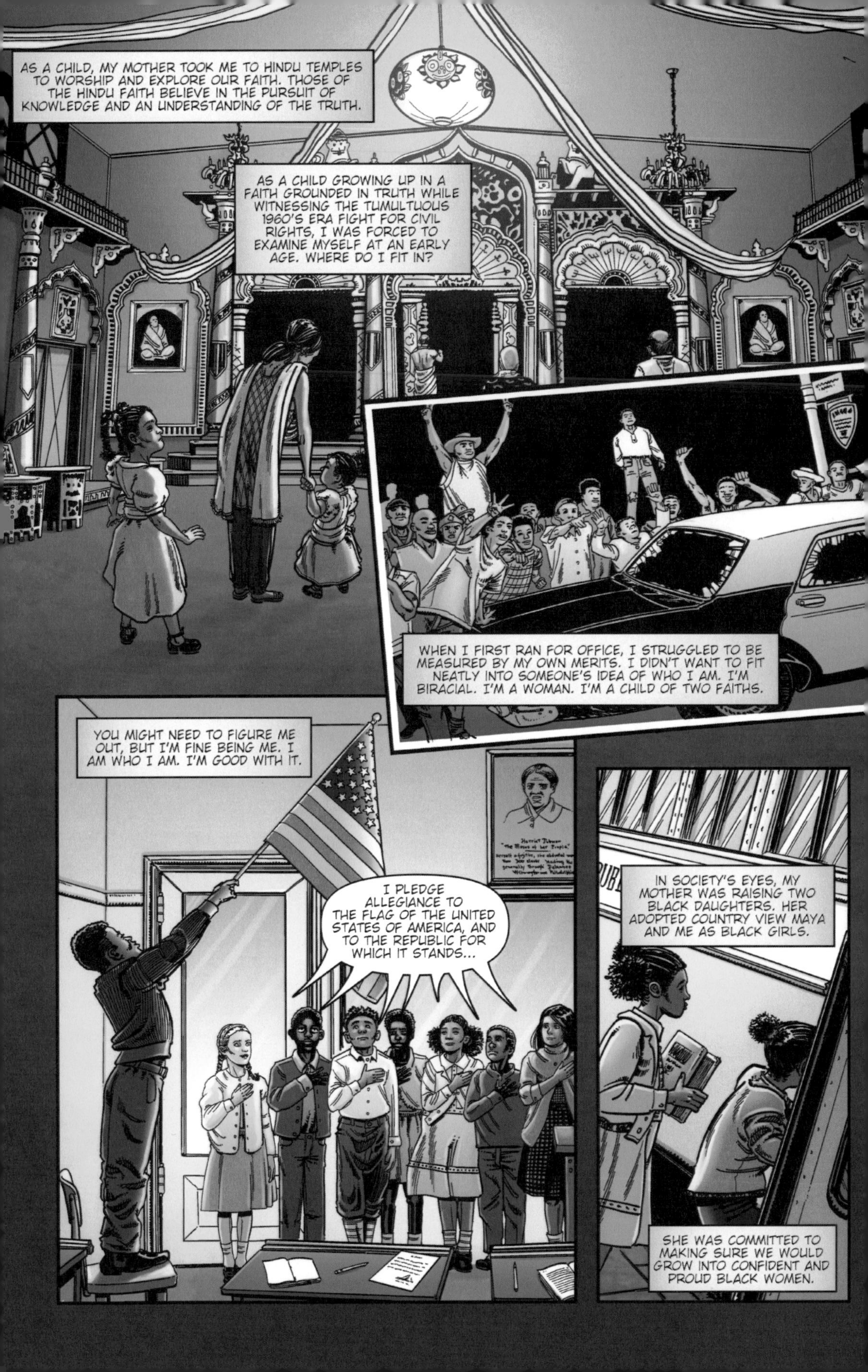
AS A CHILD, MY MOTHER TOOK ME TO HINDU TEMPLES TO WORSHIP AND EXPLORE OUR FAITH. THOSE OF THE HINDU FAITH BELIEVE IN THE PURSUIT OF KNOWLEDGE AND AN UNDERSTANDING OF THE TRUTH.
AS A CHILD GROWING UP IN A FAITH GROUNDED IN TRUTH WHILE WITNESSING THE TUMULTUOUS 1960'S ERA FIGHT FOR CIVIL RIGHTS, I WAS FORCED TO EXAMINE MYSELF AT AN EARLY AGE. WHERE DO I FIT IN?
WHEN I FIRST RAN FOR OFFICE, I STRUGGLED TO BE MEASURED BY MY OWN MERITS. I DIDN'T WANT TO FIT NEATLY INTO SOMEONE'S IDEA OF WHO I AM. I'M BIRACIAL. I'M A WOMAN. I'M A CHILD OF TWO FAITHS.
YOU MIGHT NEED TO FIGURE ME OUT, BUT I'M FINE BEING ME. I AM WHO I AM. I'M GOOD WITH IT.
I PLEDGE ALLEGIANCE TO THE FLAG OF THE UNITED STATES OF AMERICA, AND TO THE REPUBLIC FOR WHICH IT STANDS...
IN SOCIETY'S EYES, MY MOTHER WAS RAISING TWO BLACK DAUGHTERS. HER ADOPTED COUNTRY VIEW MAYA AND ME AS BLACK GIRLS.
SHE WAS COMMITTED TO MAKING SURE WE WOULD GROW INTO CONFIDENT AND PROUD BLACK WOMEN.

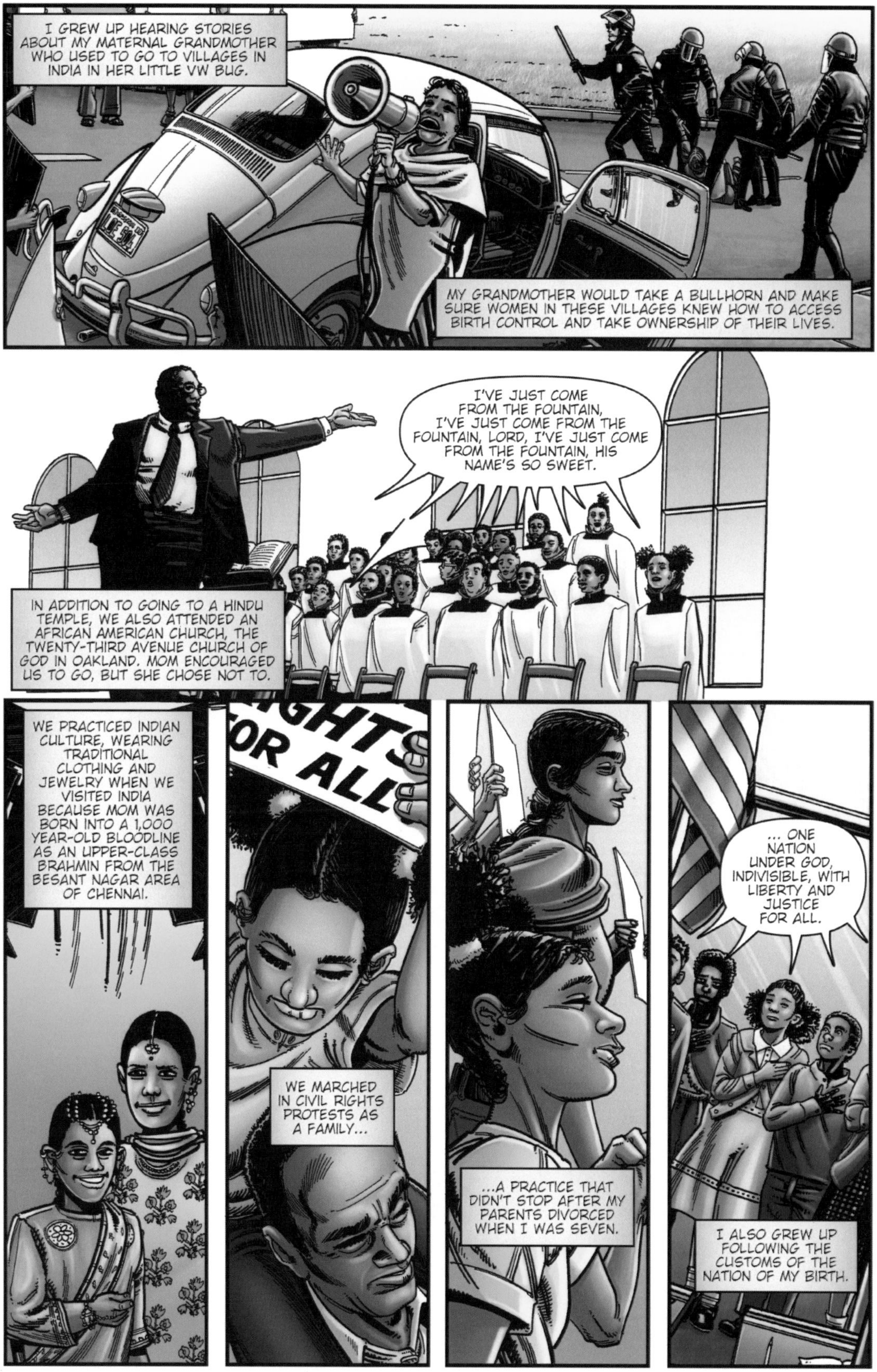
I GREW UP HEARING STORIES ABOUT MY MATERNAL GRANDMOTHER WHO USED TO GO TO VILLAGES IN INDIA IN HER LITTLE VW BUG.
MY GRANDMOTHER WOULD TAKE A BULLHORN AND MAKE SURE WOMEN IN THESE VILLAGES KNEW HOW TO ACCESS BIRTH CONTROL AND TAKE OWNERSHIP OF THEIR LIVES.
I'VE JUST COME FROM THE FOUNTAIN, I'VE JUST COME FROM THE FOUNTAIN, LORD, I'VE JUST COME FROM THE FOUNTAIN, HIS NAME'S SO SWEET.
IN ADDITION TO GOING TO A HINDU TEMPLE, WE ALSO ATTENDED AN AFRICAN AMERICAN CHURCH, THE TWENTY-THIRD AVENUE CHURCH OF GOD IN OAKLAND. MOM ENCOURAGED US TO GO, BUT SHE CHOSE NOT TO.
WE PRACTICED INDIAN CULTURE, WEARING TRADITIONAL CLOTHING AND JEWELRY WHEN WE VISITED INDIA BECAUSE MOM WAS BORN INTO A 1,000 YEAR-OLD BLOODLINE AS AN UPPER-CLASS BRAHMIN FROM THE BESANT NAGAR AREA OF CHENNAI.
WE MARCHED IN CIVIL RIGHTS PROTESTS AS A FAMILY...
...A PRACTICE THAT DIDN'T STOP AFTER MY PARENTS DIVORCED WHEN I WAS SEVEN.
... ONE NATION UNDER GOD, INDIVISIBLE, WITH LIBERTY AND JUSTICE FOR ALL.
I ALSO GREW UP FOLLOWING THE CUSTOMS OF THE NATION OF MY BIRTH.

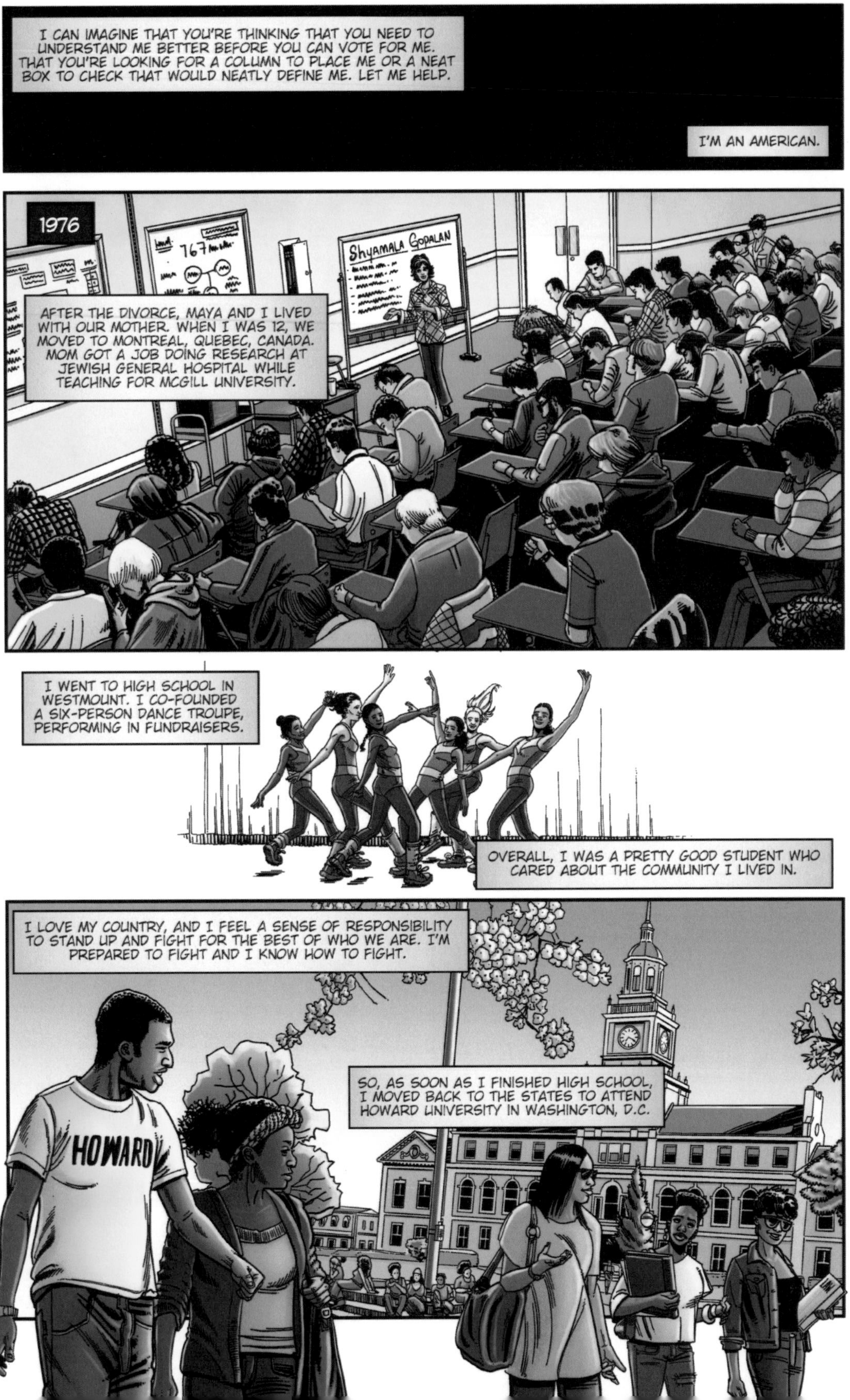
I CAN IMAGINE THAT YOU'RE THINKING THAT YOU NEED TO UNDERSTAND ME BETTER BEFORE YOU CAN VOTE FOR ME. THAT YOU'RE LOOKING FOR A COLUMN TO PLACE ME OR A NEAT BOX TO CHECK THAT WOULD NEATLY DEFINE ME. LET ME HELP.
I'M AN AMERICAN.
1976
767
Shyamala Gopalan
AFTER THE DIVORCE, MAYA AND I LIVED WITH OUR MOTHER. WHEN I WAS 12, WE MOVED TO MONTREAL, QUEBEC, CANADA. MOM GOT A JOB DOING RESEARCH AT JEWISH GENERAL HOSPITAL WHILE TEACHING FOR MCGILL UNIVERSITY.
I WENT TO HIGH SCHOOL IN WESTMOUNT. I CO-FOUNDED A SIX-PERSON DANCE TROUPE, PERFORMING IN FUNDRAISERS.
OVERALL, I WAS A PRETTY GOOD STUDENT WHO CARED ABOUT THE COMMUNITY I LIVED IN.
I LOVE MY COUNTRY, AND I FEEL A SENSE OF RESPONSIBILITY TO STAND UP AND FIGHT FOR THE BEST OF WHO WE ARE. I'M PREPARED TO FIGHT AND I KNOW HOW TO FIGHT.
SO, AS SOON AS I FINISHED HIGH SCHOOL, I MOVED BACK TO THE STATES TO ATTEND HOWARD UNIVERSITY IN WASHINGTON, D.C.
HOWARD

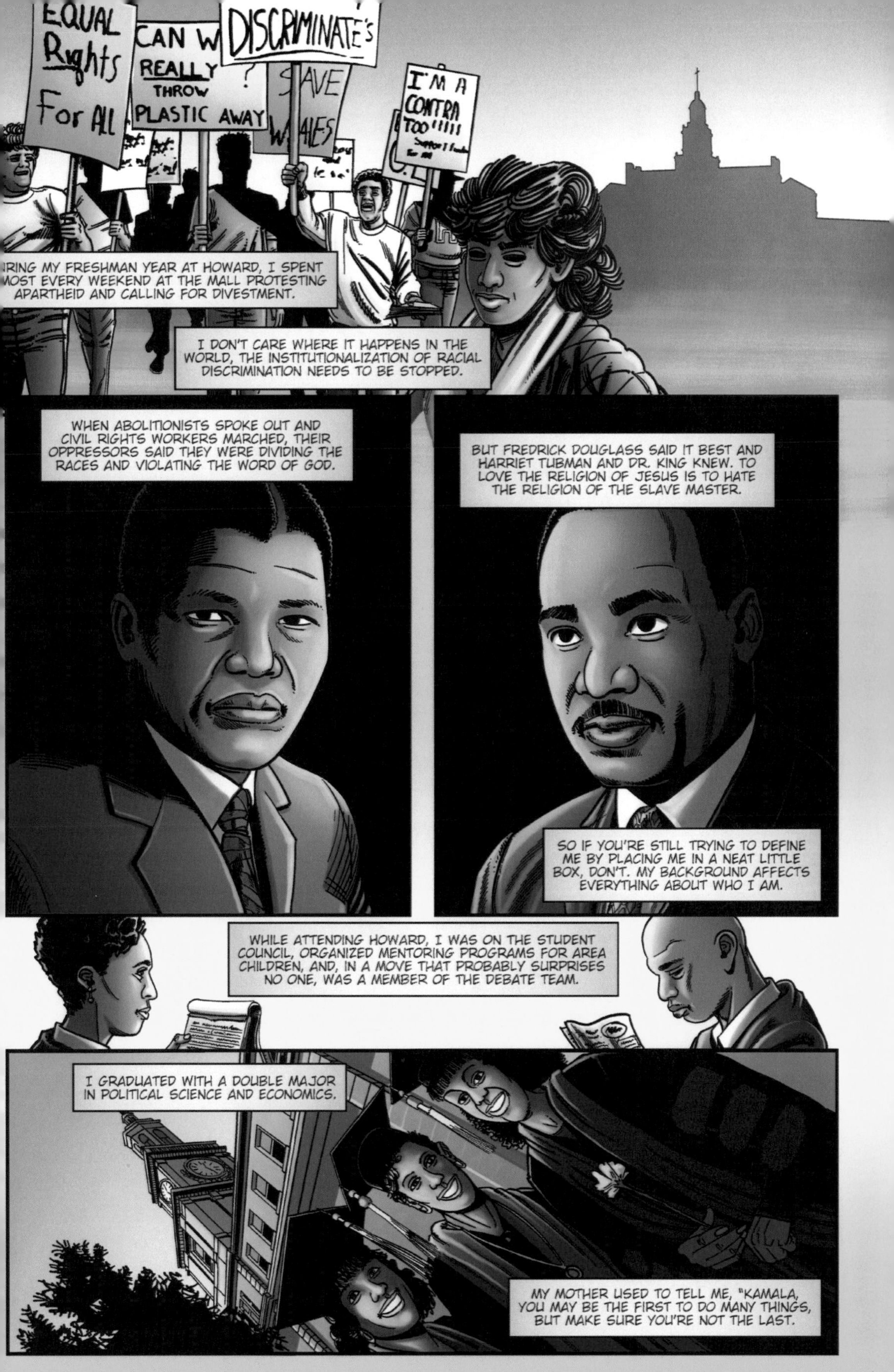
EQUAL Rights For ALL
CAN W... REALLY THROW PLASTIC AWAY ?
DISCRIMINATE's
SAVE WHALES
I'M A CONTRA TOO !!!!!!
...RING MY FRESHMAN YEAR AT HOWARD, I SPENT ...MOST EVERY WEEKEND AT THE MALL PROTESTING APARTHEID AND CALLING FOR DIVESTMENT.
I DON'T CARE WHERE IT HAPPENS IN THE WORLD, THE INSTITUTIONALIZATION OF RACIAL DISCRIMINATION NEEDS TO BE STOPPED.
WHEN ABOLITIONISTS SPOKE OUT AND CIVIL RIGHTS WORKERS MARCHED, THEIR OPPRESSORS SAID THEY WERE DIVIDING THE RACES AND VIOLATING THE WORD OF GOD.
BUT FREDRICK DOUGLASS SAID IT BEST AND HARRIET TUBMAN AND DR. KING KNEW. TO LOVE THE RELIGION OF JESUS IS TO HATE THE RELIGION OF THE SLAVE MASTER.
SO IF YOU'RE STILL TRYING TO DEFINE ME BY PLACING ME IN A NEAT LITTLE BOX, DON'T. MY BACKGROUND AFFECTS EVERYTHING ABOUT WHO I AM.
WHILE ATTENDING HOWARD, I WAS ON THE STUDENT COUNCIL, ORGANIZED MENTORING PROGRAMS FOR AREA CHILDREN, AND, IN A MOVE THAT PROBABLY SURPRISES NO ONE, WAS A MEMBER OF THE DEBATE TEAM.
I GRADUATED WITH A DOUBLE MAJOR IN POLITICAL SCIENCE AND ECONOMICS.
MY MOTHER USED TO TELL ME, "KAMALA, YOU MAY BE THE FIRST TO DO MANY THINGS, BUT MAKE SURE YOU'RE NOT THE LAST.

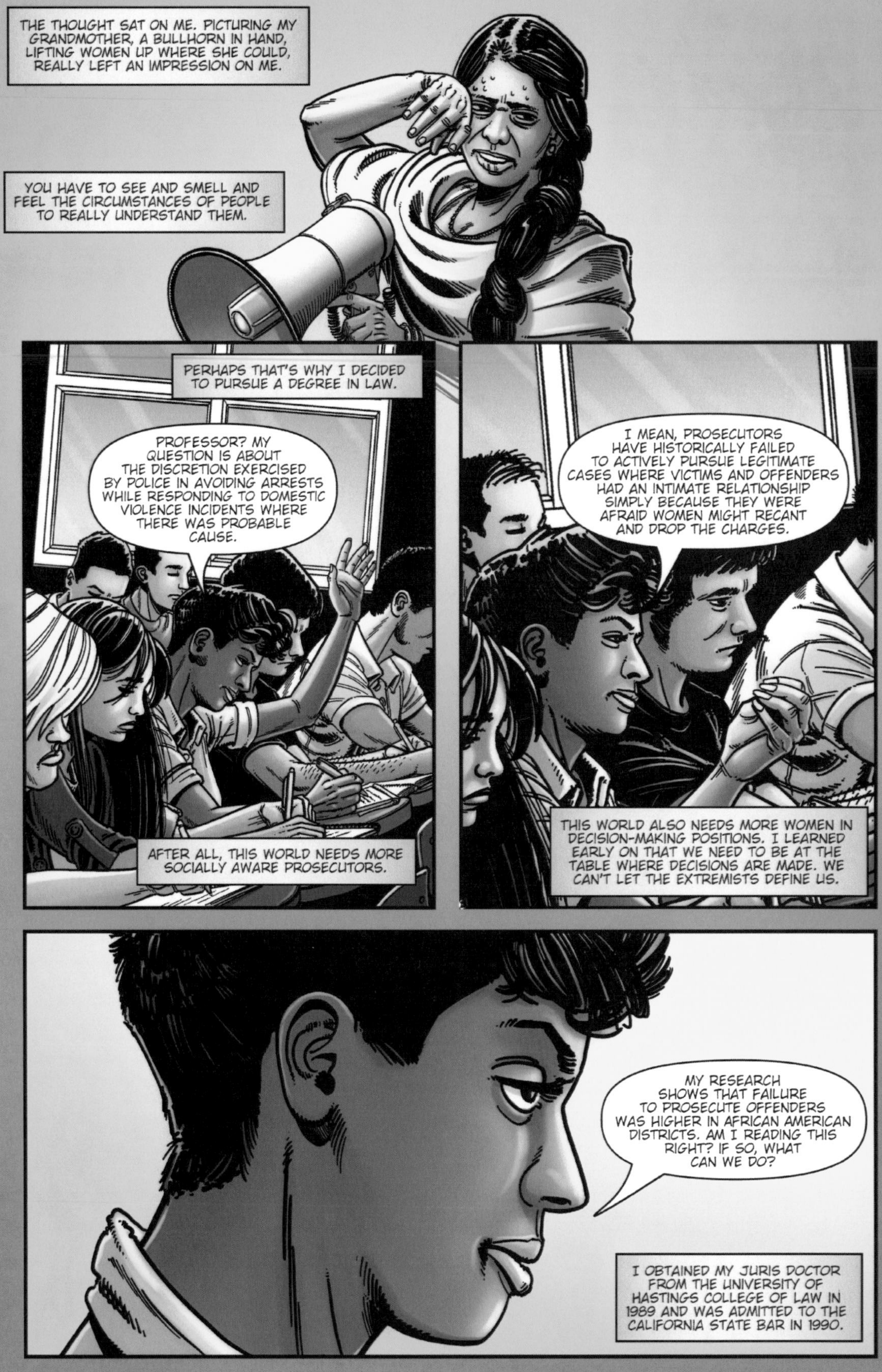
THE THOUGHT SAT ON ME. PICTURING MY GRANDMOTHER, A BULLHORN IN HAND, LIFTING WOMEN UP WHERE SHE COULD, REALLY LEFT AN IMPRESSION ON ME.
YOU HAVE TO SEE AND SMELL AND FEEL THE CIRCUMSTANCES OF PEOPLE TO REALLY UNDERSTAND THEM.
PERHAPS THAT'S WHY I DECIDED TO PURSUE A DEGREE IN LAW.
PROFESSOR? MY QUESTION IS ABOUT THE DISCRETION EXERCISED BY POLICE IN AVOIDING ARRESTS WHILE RESPONDING TO DOMESTIC VIOLENCE INCIDENTS WHERE THERE WAS PROBABLE CAUSE.
AFTER ALL, THIS WORLD NEEDS MORE SOCIALLY AWARE PROSECUTORS.
I MEAN, PROSECUTORS HAVE HISTORICALLY FAILED TO ACTIVELY PURSUE LEGITIMATE CASES WHERE VICTIMS AND OFFENDERS HAD AN INTIMATE RELATIONSHIP SIMPLY BECAUSE THEY WERE AFRAID WOMEN MIGHT RECANT AND DROP THE CHARGES.
THIS WORLD ALSO NEEDS MORE WOMEN IN DECISION-MAKING POSITIONS. I LEARNED EARLY ON THAT WE NEED TO BE AT THE TABLE WHERE DECISIONS ARE MADE. WE CAN'T LET THE EXTREMISTS DEFINE US.
MY RESEARCH SHOWS THAT FAILURE TO PROSECUTE OFFENDERS WAS HIGHER IN AFRICAN AMERICAN DISTRICTS. AM I READING THIS RIGHT? IF SO, WHAT CAN WE DO?
I OBTAINED MY JURIS DOCTOR FROM THE UNIVERSITY OF HASTINGS COLLEGE OF LAW IN 1989 AND WAS ADMITTED TO THE CALIFORNIA STATE BAR IN 1990.

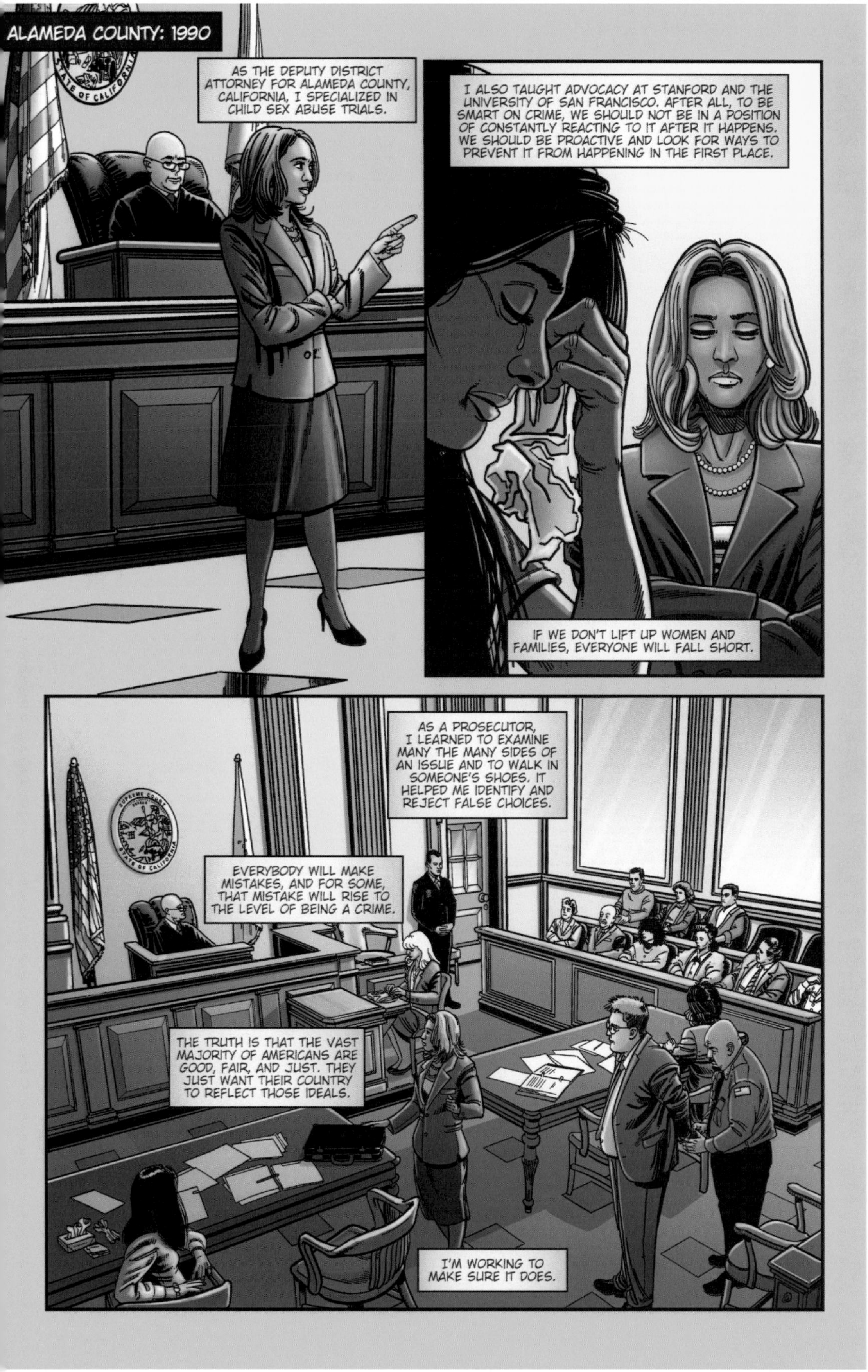

ALAMEDA COUNTY: 1990
AS THE DEPUTY DISTRICT ATTORNEY FOR ALAMEDA COUNTY, CALIFORNIA, I SPECIALIZED IN CHILD SEX ABUSE TRIALS.
I ALSO TAUGHT ADVOCACY AT STANFORD AND THE UNIVERSITY OF SAN FRANCISCO. AFTER ALL, TO BE SMART ON CRIME, WE SHOULD NOT BE IN A POSITION OF CONSTANTLY REACTING TO IT AFTER IT HAPPENS. WE SHOULD BE PROACTIVE AND LOOK FOR WAYS TO PREVENT IT FROM HAPPENING IN THE FIRST PLACE.
IF WE DON'T LIFT UP WOMEN AND FAMILIES, EVERYONE WILL FALL SHORT.
AS A PROSECUTOR, I LEARNED TO EXAMINE MANY THE MANY SIDES OF AN ISSUE AND TO WALK IN SOMEONE'S SHOES. IT HELPED ME IDENTIFY AND REJECT FALSE CHOICES.
EVERYBODY WILL MAKE MISTAKES, AND FOR SOME, THAT MISTAKE WILL RISE TO THE LEVEL OF BEING A CRIME.
THE TRUTH IS THAT THE VAST MAJORITY OF AMERICANS ARE GOOD, FAIR, AND JUST. THEY JUST WANT THEIR COUNTRY TO REFLECT THOSE IDEALS.
I'M WORKING TO MAKE SURE IT DOES.

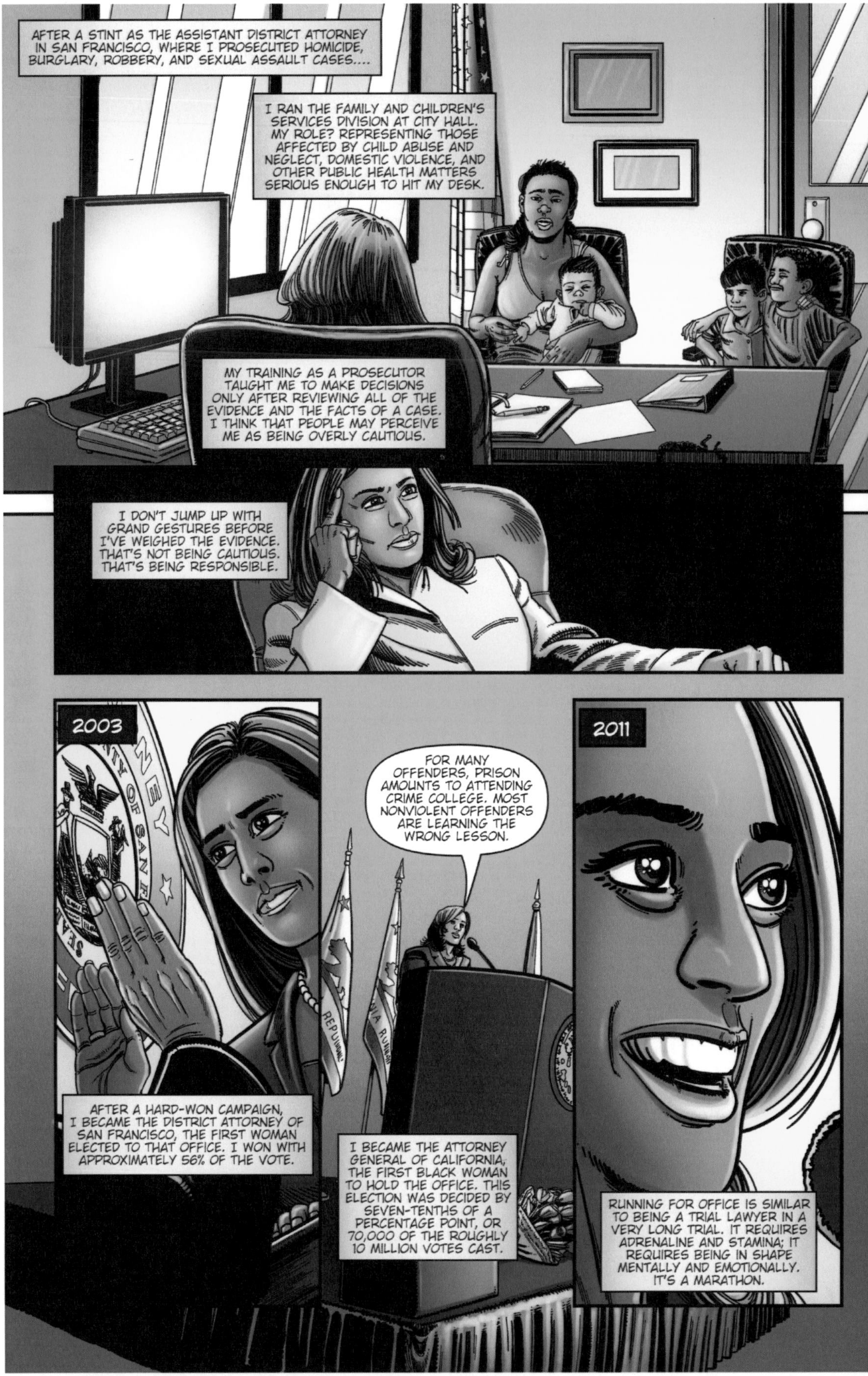
AFTER A STINT AS THE ASSISTANT DISTRICT ATTORNEY IN SAN FRANCISCO, WHERE I PROSECUTED HOMICIDE, BURGLARY, ROBBERY, AND SEXUAL ASSAULT CASES....
I RAN THE FAMILY AND CHILDREN'S SERVICES DIVISION AT CITY HALL. MY ROLE? REPRESENTING THOSE AFFECTED BY CHILD ABUSE AND NEGLECT, DOMESTIC VIOLENCE, AND OTHER PUBLIC HEALTH MATTERS SERIOUS ENOUGH TO HIT MY DESK.
MY TRAINING AS A PROSECUTOR TAUGHT ME TO MAKE DECISIONS ONLY AFTER REVIEWING ALL OF THE EVIDENCE AND THE FACTS OF A CASE. I THINK THAT PEOPLE MAY PERCEIVE ME AS BEING OVERLY CAUTIOUS.
I DON'T JUMP UP WITH GRAND GESTURES BEFORE I'VE WEIGHED THE EVIDENCE. THAT'S NOT BEING CAUTIOUS. THAT'S BEING RESPONSIBLE.
2003
AFTER A HARD-WON CAMPAIGN, I BECAME THE DISTRICT ATTORNEY OF SAN FRANCISCO, THE FIRST WOMAN ELECTED TO THAT OFFICE. I WON WITH APPROXIMATELY 56% OF THE VOTE.
FOR MANY OFFENDERS, PRISON AMOUNTS TO ATTENDING CRIME COLLEGE. MOST NONVIOLENT OFFENDERS ARE LEARNING THE WRONG LESSON.
I BECAME THE ATTORNEY GENERAL OF CALIFORNIA, THE FIRST BLACK WOMAN TO HOLD THE OFFICE. THIS ELECTION WAS DECIDED BY SEVEN-TENTHS OF A PERCENTAGE POINT, OR 70,000 OF THE ROUGHLY 10 MILLION VOTES CAST.
2011
RUNNING FOR OFFICE IS SIMILAR TO BEING A TRIAL LAWYER IN A VERY LONG TRIAL. IT REQUIRES ADRENALINE AND STAMINA; IT REQUIRES BEING IN SHAPE MENTALLY AND EMOTIONALLY. IT'S A MARATHON.

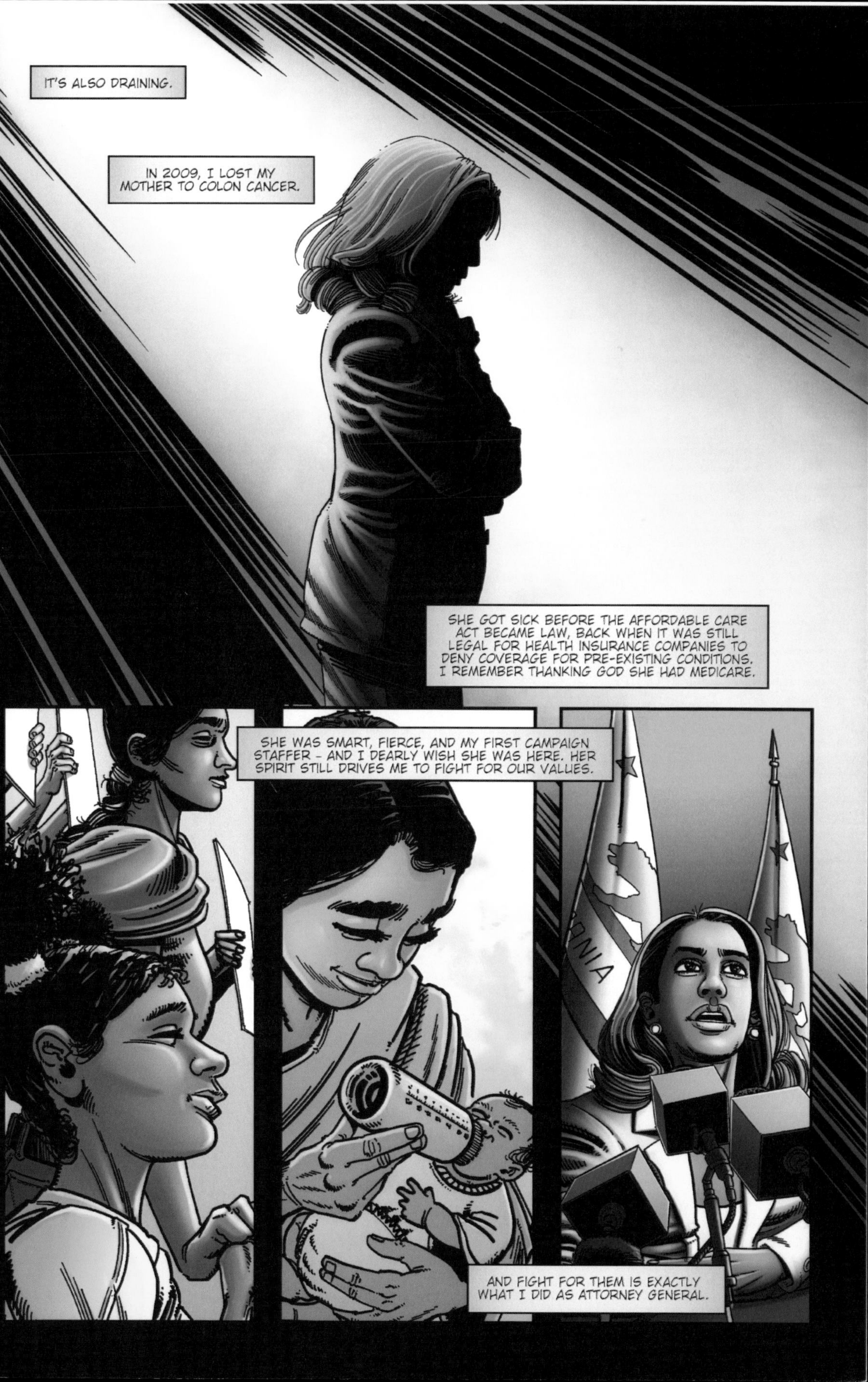
IT'S ALSO DRAINING.
IN 2009, I LOST MY MOTHER TO COLON CANCER.
SHE GOT SICK BEFORE THE AFFORDABLE CARE ACT BECAME LAW, BACK WHEN IT WAS STILL LEGAL FOR HEALTH INSURANCE COMPANIES TO DENY COVERAGE FOR PRE-EXISTING CONDITIONS. I REMEMBER THANKING GOD SHE HAD MEDICARE.
SHE WAS SMART, FIERCE, AND MY FIRST CAMPAIGN STAFFER - AND I DEARLY WISH SHE WAS HERE. HER SPIRIT STILL DRIVES ME TO FIGHT FOR OUR VALUES.
AND FIGHT FOR THEM IS EXACTLY WHAT I DID AS ATTORNEY GENERAL.

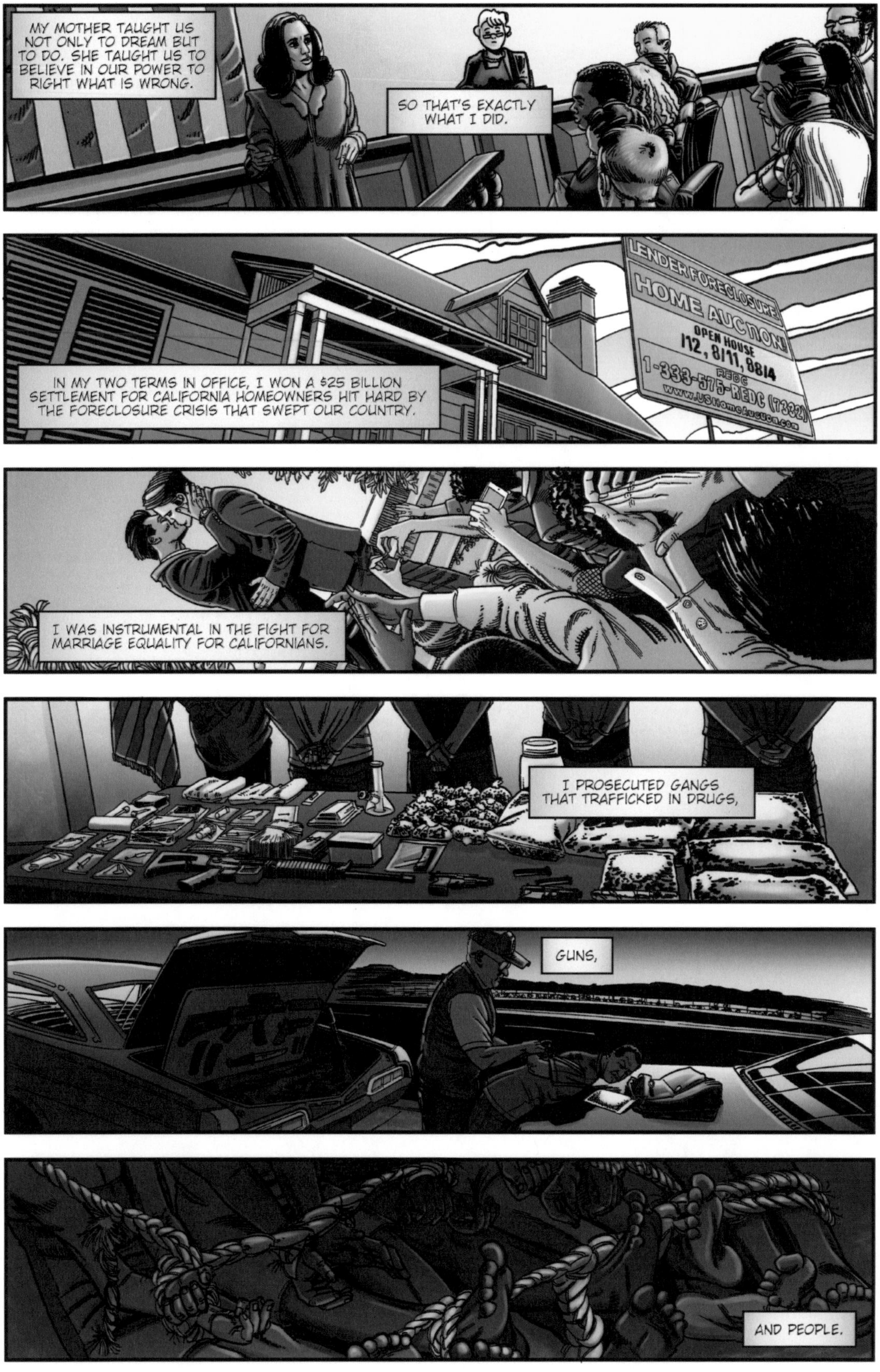

MY MOTHER TAUGHT US NOT ONLY TO DREAM BUT TO DO. SHE TAUGHT US TO BELIEVE IN OUR POWER TO RIGHT WHAT IS WRONG.
SO THAT'S EXACTLY WHAT I DID.
LENDER FORECLOSURE!
HOME AUCTION!
OPEN HOUSE
IN MY TWO TERMS IN OFFICE, I WON A $25 BILLION SETTLEMENT FOR CALIFORNIA HOMEOWNERS HIT HARD BY THE FORECLOSURE CRISIS THAT SWEPT OUR COUNTRY.
I WAS INSTRUMENTAL IN THE FIGHT FOR MARRIAGE EQUALITY FOR CALIFORNIANS.
I PROSECUTED GANGS THAT TRAFFICKED IN DRUGS,
GUNS,
AND PEOPLE.

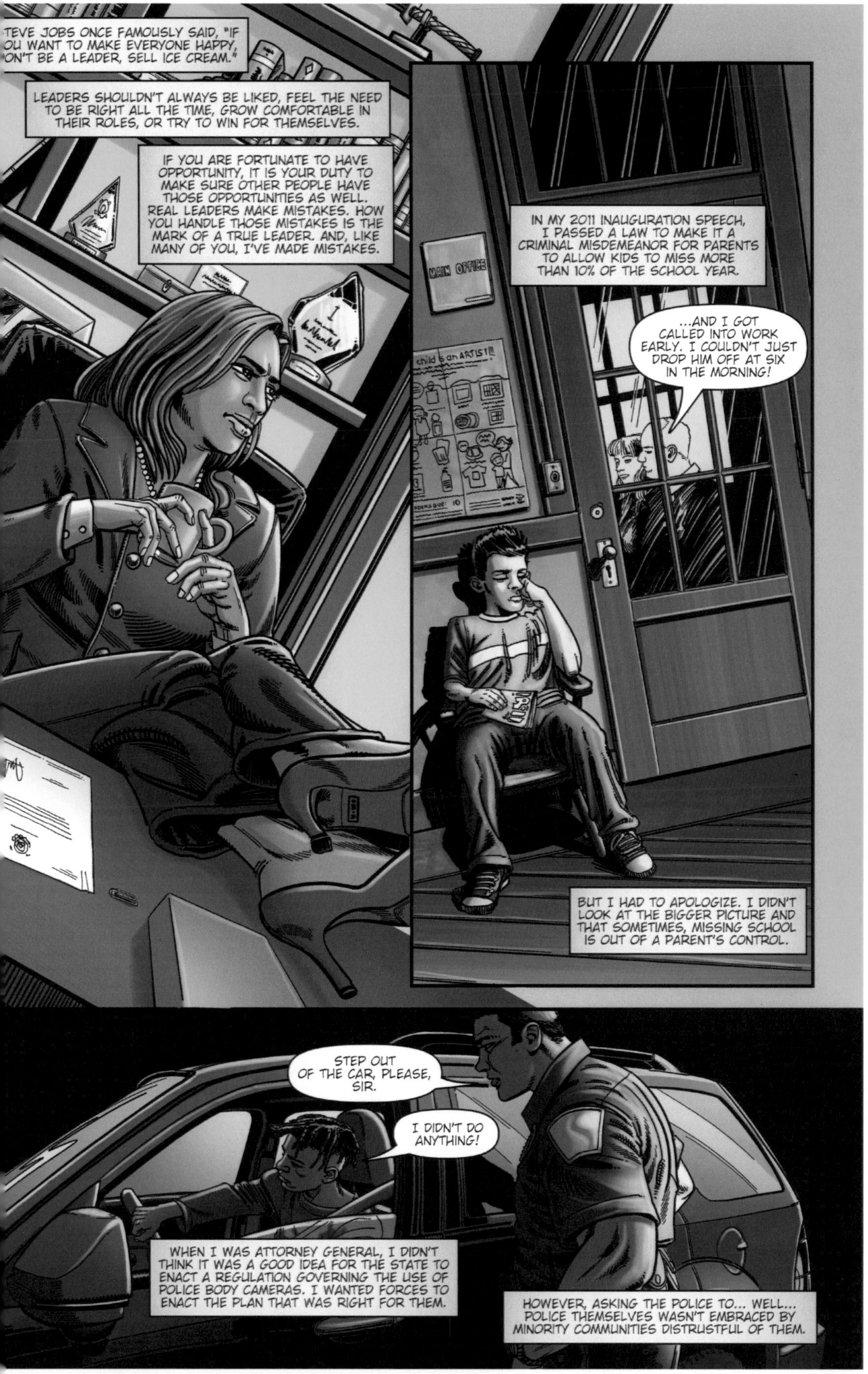

STEVE JOBS ONCE FAMOUSLY SAID, "IF YOU WANT TO MAKE EVERYONE HAPPY, DON'T BE A LEADER, SELL ICE CREAM."
LEADERS SHOULDN'T ALWAYS BE LIKED, FEEL THE NEED TO BE RIGHT ALL THE TIME, GROW COMFORTABLE IN THEIR ROLES, OR TRY TO WIN FOR THEMSELVES.
IF YOU ARE FORTUNATE TO HAVE OPPORTUNITY, IT IS YOUR DUTY TO MAKE SURE OTHER PEOPLE HAVE THOSE OPPORTUNITIES AS WELL. REAL LEADERS MAKE MISTAKES. HOW YOU HANDLE THOSE MISTAKES IS THE MARK OF A TRUE LEADER. AND, LIKE MANY OF YOU, I'VE MADE MISTAKES.
IN MY 2011 INAUGURATION SPEECH, I PASSED A LAW TO MAKE IT A CRIMINAL MISDEMEANOR FOR PARENTS TO ALLOW KIDS TO MISS MORE THAN 10% OF THE SCHOOL YEAR.
MAIN OFFICE
...AND I GOT CALLED INTO WORK EARLY. I COULDN'T JUST DROP HIM OFF AT SIX IN THE MORNING!
BUT I HAD TO APOLOGIZE. I DIDN'T LOOK AT THE BIGGER PICTURE AND THAT SOMETIMES, MISSING SCHOOL IS OUT OF A PARENT'S CONTROL.
STEP OUT OF THE CAR, PLEASE, SIR.
I DIDN'T DO ANYTHING!
WHEN I WAS ATTORNEY GENERAL, I DIDN'T THINK IT WAS A GOOD IDEA FOR THE STATE TO ENACT A REGULATION GOVERNING THE USE OF POLICE BODY CAMERAS. I WANTED FORCES TO ENACT THE PLAN THAT WAS RIGHT FOR THEM.
HOWEVER, ASKING THE POLICE TO... WELL... POLICE THEMSELVES WASN'T EMBRACED BY MINORITY COMMUNITIES DISTRUSTFUL OF THEM.

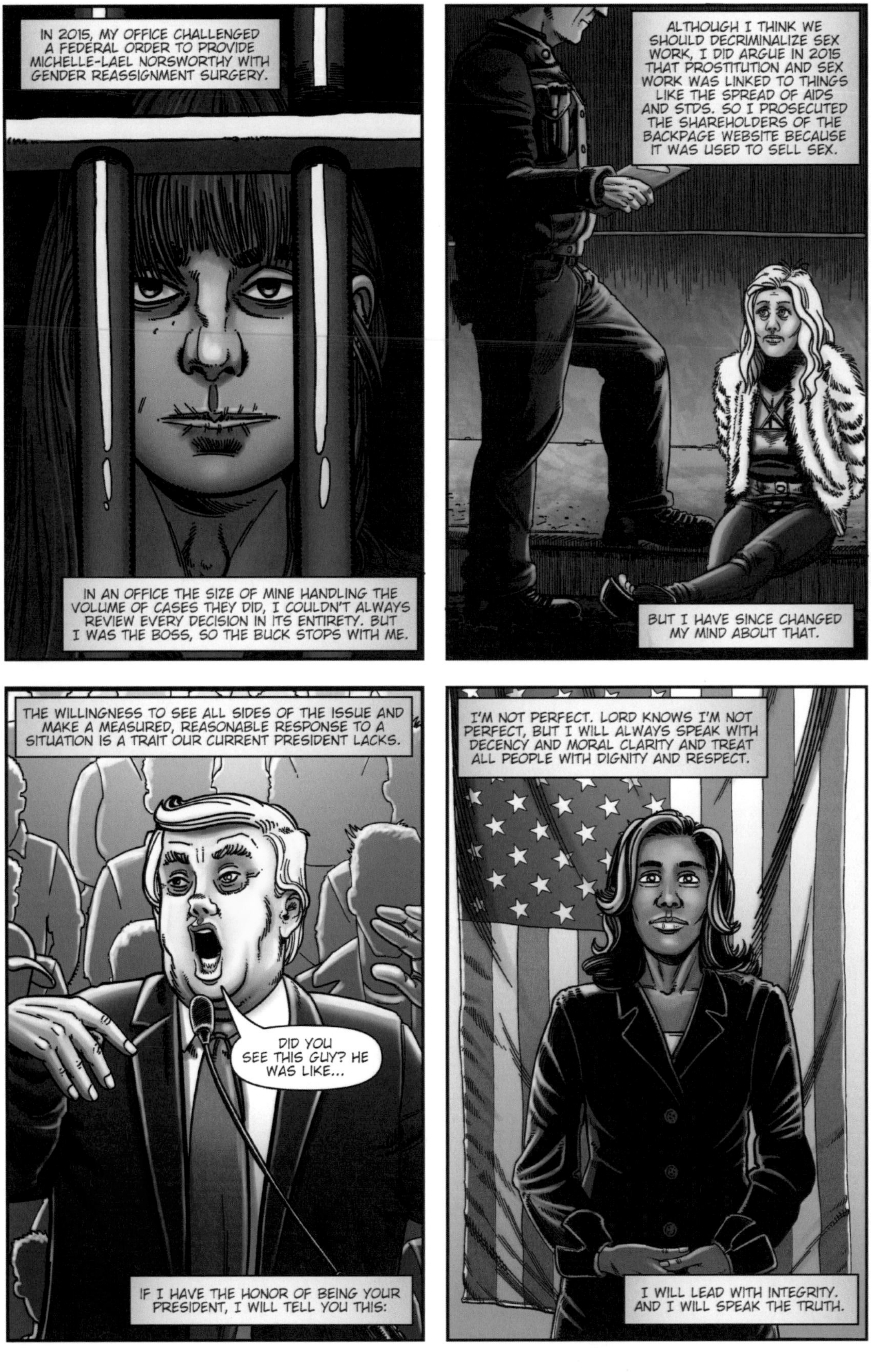
IN 2015, MY OFFICE CHALLENGED A FEDERAL ORDER TO PROVIDE MICHELLE-LAEL NORSWORTHY WITH GENDER REASSIGNMENT SURGERY.
IN AN OFFICE THE SIZE OF MINE HANDLING THE VOLUME OF CASES THEY DID, I COULDN'T ALWAYS REVIEW EVERY DECISION IN ITS ENTIRETY. BUT I WAS THE BOSS, SO THE BUCK STOPS WITH ME.
ALTHOUGH I THINK WE SHOULD DECRIMINALIZE SEX WORK, I DID ARGUE IN 2015 THAT PROSTITUTION AND SEX WORK WAS LINKED TO THINGS LIKE THE SPREAD OF AIDS AND STDS. SO I PROSECUTED THE SHAREHOLDERS OF THE BACKPAGE WEBSITE BECAUSE IT WAS USED TO SELL SEX.
BUT I HAVE SINCE CHANGED MY MIND ABOUT THAT.
THE WILLINGNESS TO SEE ALL SIDES OF THE ISSUE AND MAKE A MEASURED, REASONABLE RESPONSE TO A SITUATION IS A TRAIT OUR CURRENT PRESIDENT LACKS.
DID YOU SEE THIS GUY? HE WAS LIKE...
IF I HAVE THE HONOR OF BEING YOUR PRESIDENT, I WILL TELL YOU THIS:
I'M NOT PERFECT. LORD KNOWS I'M NOT PERFECT, BUT I WILL ALWAYS SPEAK WITH DECENCY AND MORAL CLARITY AND TREAT ALL PEOPLE WITH DIGNITY AND RESPECT.
I WILL LEAD WITH INTEGRITY. AND I WILL SPEAK THE TRUTH.

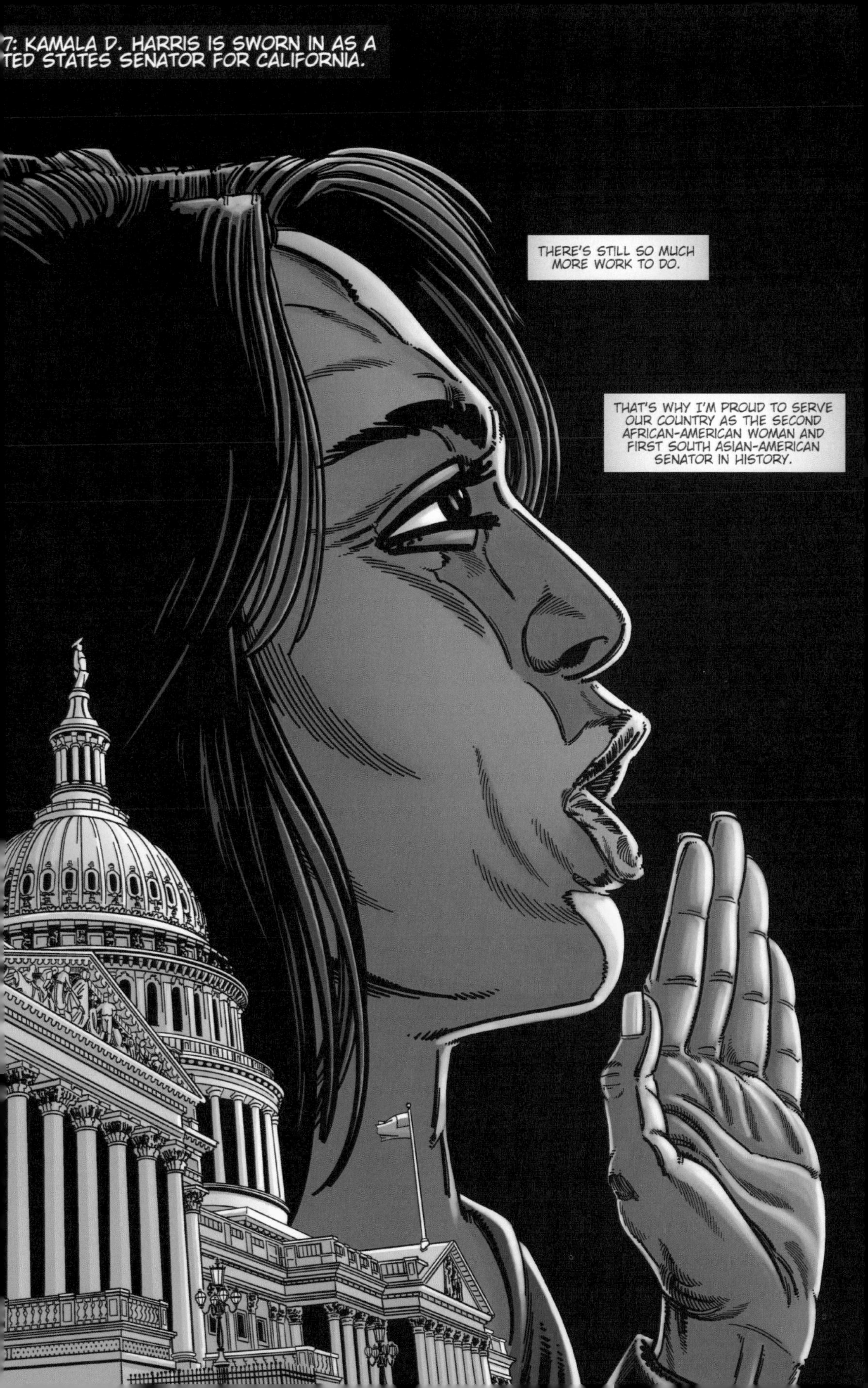
7: KAMALA D. HARRIS IS SWORN IN AS A TED STATES SENATOR FOR CALIFORNIA.
THERE'S STILL SO MUCH MORE WORK TO DO.
THAT'S WHY I'M PROUD TO SERVE OUR COUNTRY AS THE SECOND AFRICAN-AMERICAN WOMAN AND FIRST SOUTH ASIAN-AMERICAN SENATOR IN HISTORY.

FEBRUARY 11, 2019: "THE BREAKFAST CLUB" MORNING SHOW

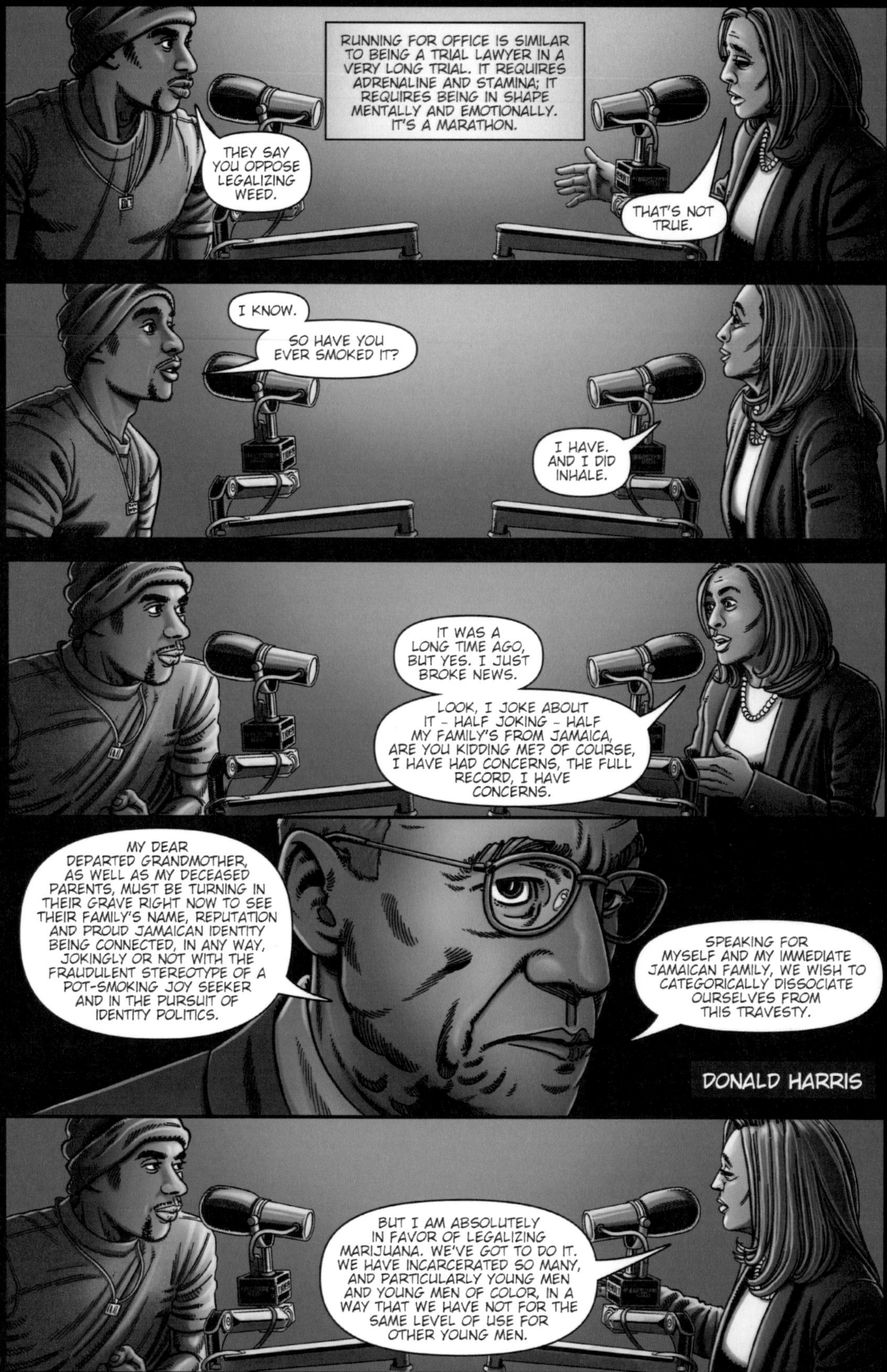
RUNNING FOR OFFICE IS SIMILAR TO BEING A TRIAL LAWYER IN A VERY LONG TRIAL. IT REQUIRES ADRENALINE AND STAMINA; IT REQUIRES BEING IN SHAPE MENTALLY AND EMOTIONALLY. IT'S A MARATHON.
THEY SAY YOU OPPOSE LEGALIZING WEED.
THAT'S NOT TRUE.
I KNOW.
SO HAVE YOU EVER SMOKED IT?
I HAVE. AND I DID INHALE.
IT WAS A LONG TIME AGO, BUT YES. I JUST BROKE NEWS.
LOOK, I JOKE ABOUT IT - HALF JOKING - HALF MY FAMILY'S FROM JAMAICA, ARE YOU KIDDING ME? OF COURSE, I HAVE HAD CONCERNS, THE FULL RECORD, I HAVE CONCERNS.
MY DEAR DEPARTED GRANDMOTHER, AS WELL AS MY DECEASED PARENTS, MUST BE TURNING IN THEIR GRAVE RIGHT NOW TO SEE THEIR FAMILY'S NAME, REPUTATION AND PROUD JAMAICAN IDENTITY BEING CONNECTED, IN ANY WAY, JOKINGLY OR NOT WITH THE FRAUDULENT STEREOTYPE OF A POT-SMOKING JOY SEEKER AND IN THE PURSUIT OF IDENTITY POLITICS.
SPEAKING FOR MYSELF AND MY IMMEDIATE JAMAICAN FAMILY, WE WISH TO CATEGORICALLY DISSOCIATE OURSELVES FROM THIS TRAVESTY.
DONALD HARRIS
BUT I AM ABSOLUTELY IN FAVOR OF LEGALIZING MARIJUANA. WE'VE GOT TO DO IT. WE HAVE INCARCERATED SO MANY, AND PARTICULARLY YOUNG MEN AND YOUNG MEN OF COLOR, IN A WAY THAT WE HAVE NOT FOR THE SAME LEVEL OF USE FOR OTHER YOUNG MEN.

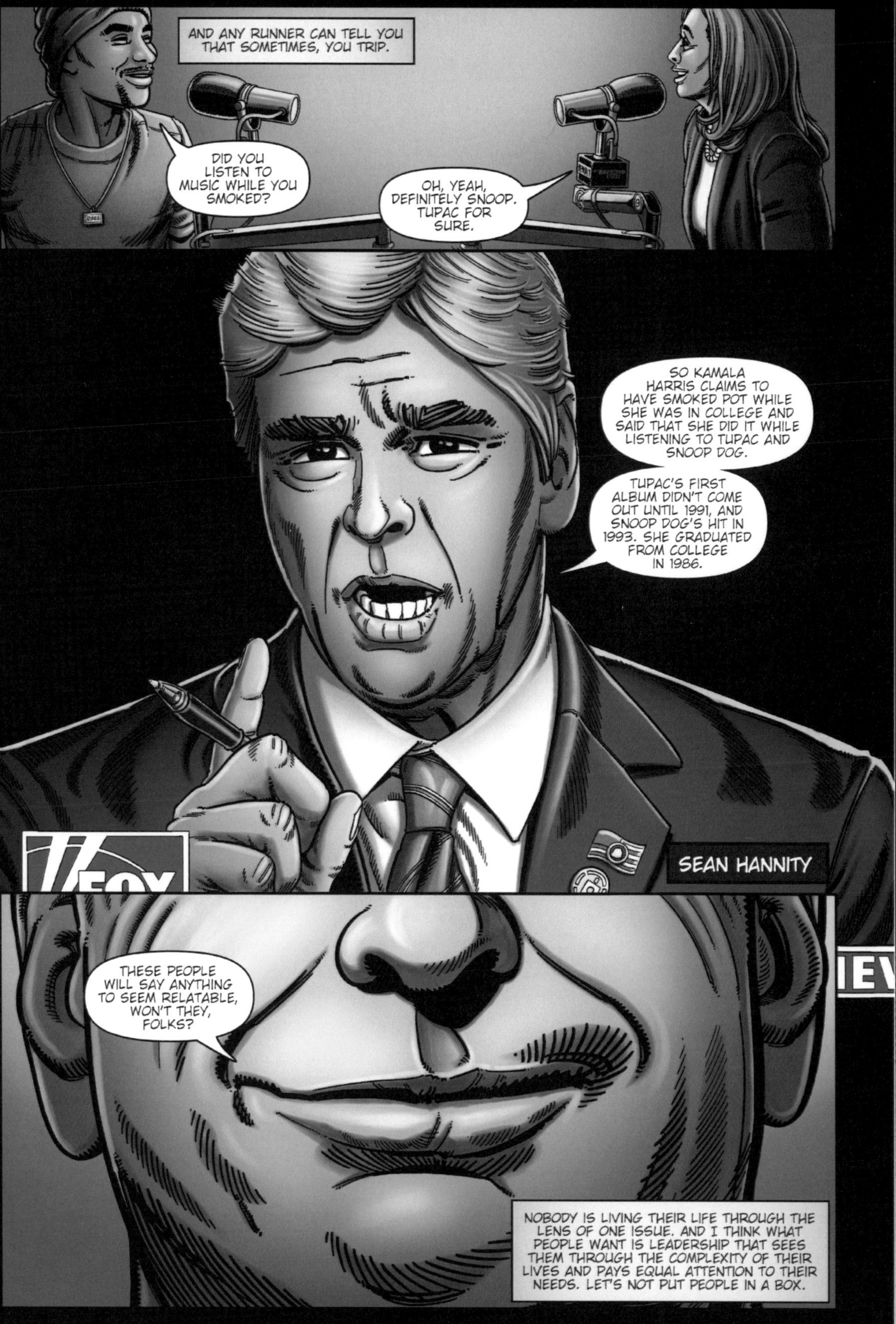
AND ANY RUNNER CAN TELL YOU THAT SOMETIMES, YOU TRIP.
DID YOU LISTEN TO MUSIC WHILE YOU SMOKED?
OH, YEAH, DEFINITELY SNOOP. TUPAC FOR SURE.
SO KAMALA HARRIS CLAIMS TO HAVE SMOKED POT WHILE SHE WAS IN COLLEGE AND SAID THAT SHE DID IT WHILE LISTENING TO TUPAC AND SNOOP DOG.
TUPAC'S FIRST ALBUM DIDN'T COME OUT UNTIL 1991, AND SNOOP DOG'S HIT IN 1993. SHE GRADUATED FROM COLLEGE IN 1986.
SEAN HANNITY
THESE PEOPLE WILL SAY ANYTHING TO SEEM RELATABLE, WON'T THEY, FOLKS?
NOBODY IS LIVING THEIR LIFE THROUGH THE LENS OF ONE ISSUE. AND I THINK WHAT PEOPLE WANT IS LEADERSHIP THAT SEES THEM THROUGH THE COMPLEXITY OF THEIR LIVES AND PAYS EQUAL ATTENTION TO THEIR NEEDS. LET'S NOT PUT PEOPLE IN A BOX.

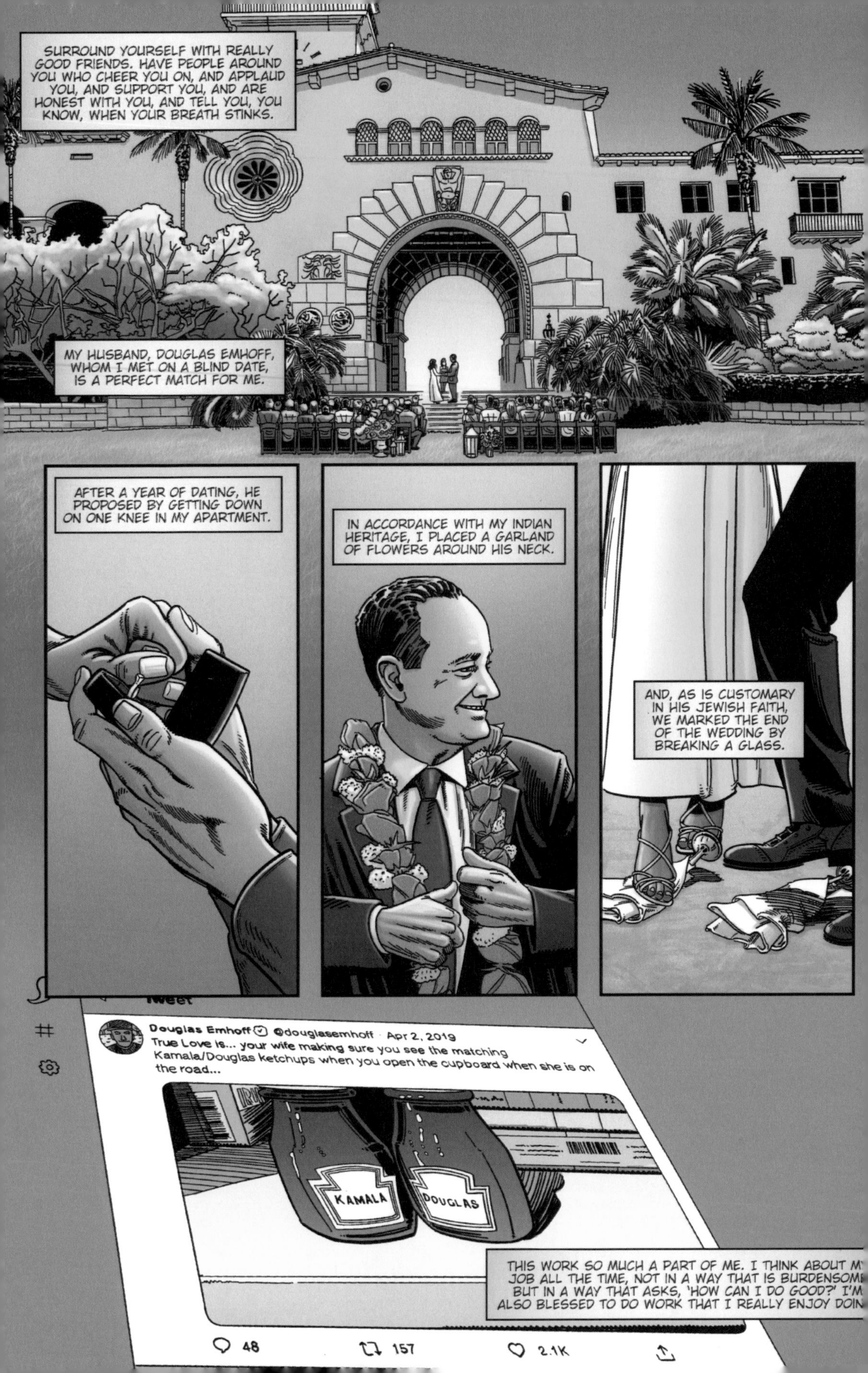

SURROUND YOURSELF WITH REALLY GOOD FRIENDS. HAVE PEOPLE AROUND YOU WHO CHEER YOU ON, AND APPLAUD YOU, AND SUPPORT YOU, AND ARE HONEST WITH YOU, AND TELL YOU, YOU KNOW, WHEN YOUR BREATH STINKS.
MY HUSBAND, DOUGLAS EMHOFF, WHOM I MET ON A BLIND DATE, IS A PERFECT MATCH FOR ME.
AFTER A YEAR OF DATING, HE PROPOSED BY GETTING DOWN ON ONE KNEE IN MY APARTMENT.
IN ACCORDANCE WITH MY INDIAN HERITAGE, I PLACED A GARLAND OF FLOWERS AROUND HIS NECK.
AND, AS IS CUSTOMARY IN HIS JEWISH FAITH, WE MARKED THE END OF THE WEDDING BY BREAKING A GLASS.
Tweet
Douglas Emhoff @douglasemhoff · Apr 2, 2019
True Love is... your wife making sure you see the matching Kamala/Douglas ketchups when you open the cupboard when she is on the road...
KAMALA
DOUGLAS
48
157
2.1K
THIS WORK SO MUCH A PART OF ME. I THINK ABOUT M
JOB ALL THE TIME, NOT IN A WAY THAT IS BURDENSOM
BUT IN A WAY THAT ASKS, 'HOW CAN I DO GOOD?' I'M
ALSO BLESSED TO DO WORK THAT I REALLY ENJOY DOIN

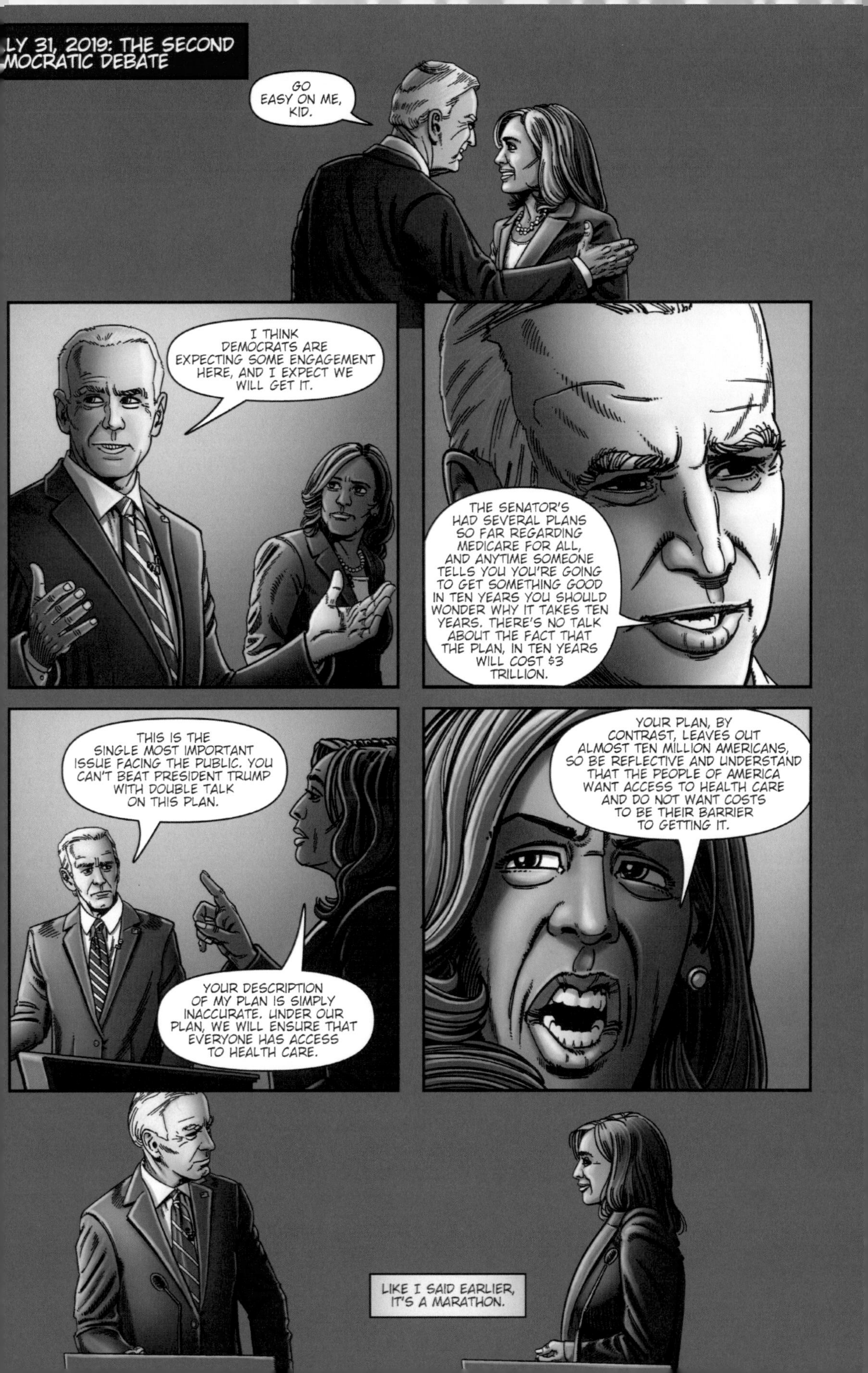

LY 31, 2019: THE SECOND MOCRATIC DEBATE
GO EASY ON ME, KID.
I THINK DEMOCRATS ARE EXPECTING SOME ENGAGEMENT HERE, AND I EXPECT WE WILL GET IT.
THE SENATOR'S HAD SEVERAL PLANS SO FAR REGARDING MEDICARE FOR ALL, AND ANYTIME SOMEONE TELLS YOU YOU'RE GOING TO GET SOMETHING GOOD IN TEN YEARS YOU SHOULD WONDER WHY IT TAKES TEN YEARS. THERE'S NO TALK ABOUT THE FACT THAT THE PLAN, IN TEN YEARS WILL COST $3 TRILLION.
THIS IS THE SINGLE MOST IMPORTANT ISSUE FACING THE PUBLIC. YOU CAN'T BEAT PRESIDENT TRUMP WITH DOUBLE TALK ON THIS PLAN.
YOUR DESCRIPTION OF MY PLAN IS SIMPLY INACCURATE. UNDER OUR PLAN, WE WILL ENSURE THAT EVERYONE HAS ACCESS TO HEALTH CARE.
YOUR PLAN, BY CONTRAST, LEAVES OUT ALMOST TEN MILLION AMERICANS, SO BE REFLECTIVE AND UNDERSTAND THAT THE PEOPLE OF AMERICA WANT ACCESS TO HEALTH CARE AND DO NOT WANT COSTS TO BE THEIR BARRIER TO GETTING IT.
LIKE I SAID EARLIER, IT'S A MARATHON.

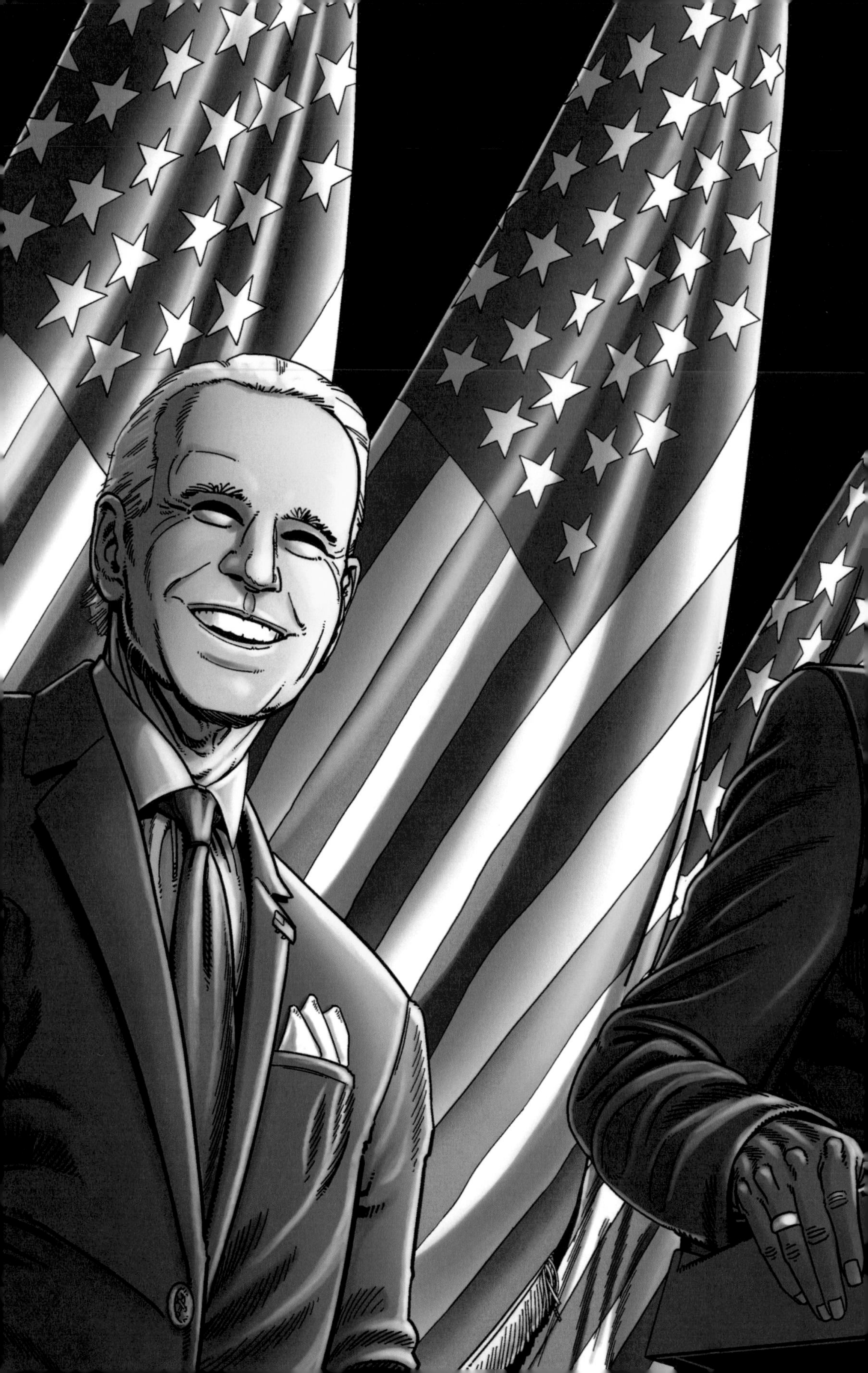

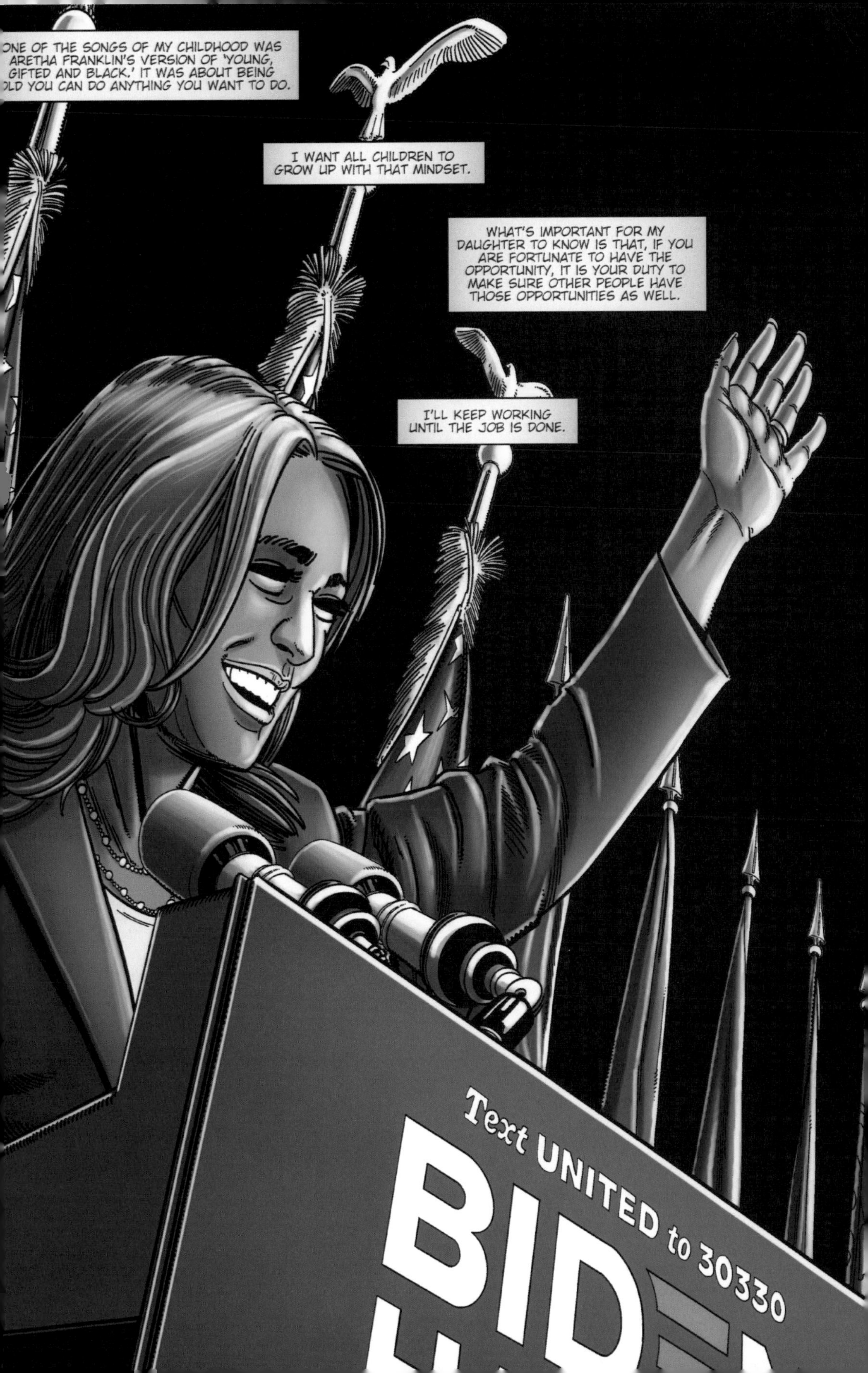
ONE OF THE SONGS OF MY CHILDHOOD WAS ARETHA FRANKLIN'S VERSION OF 'YOUNG, GIFTED AND BLACK.' IT WAS ABOUT BEING TOLD YOU CAN DO ANYTHING YOU WANT TO DO.
I WANT ALL CHILDREN TO GROW UP WITH THAT MINDSET.
WHAT'S IMPORTANT FOR MY DAUGHTER TO KNOW IS THAT, IF YOU ARE FORTUNATE TO HAVE THE OPPORTUNITY, IT IS YOUR DUTY TO MAKE SURE OTHER PEOPLE HAVE THOSE OPPORTUNITIES AS WELL.
I'LL KEEP WORKING UNTIL THE JOB IS DONE.
Text UNITED to 30330

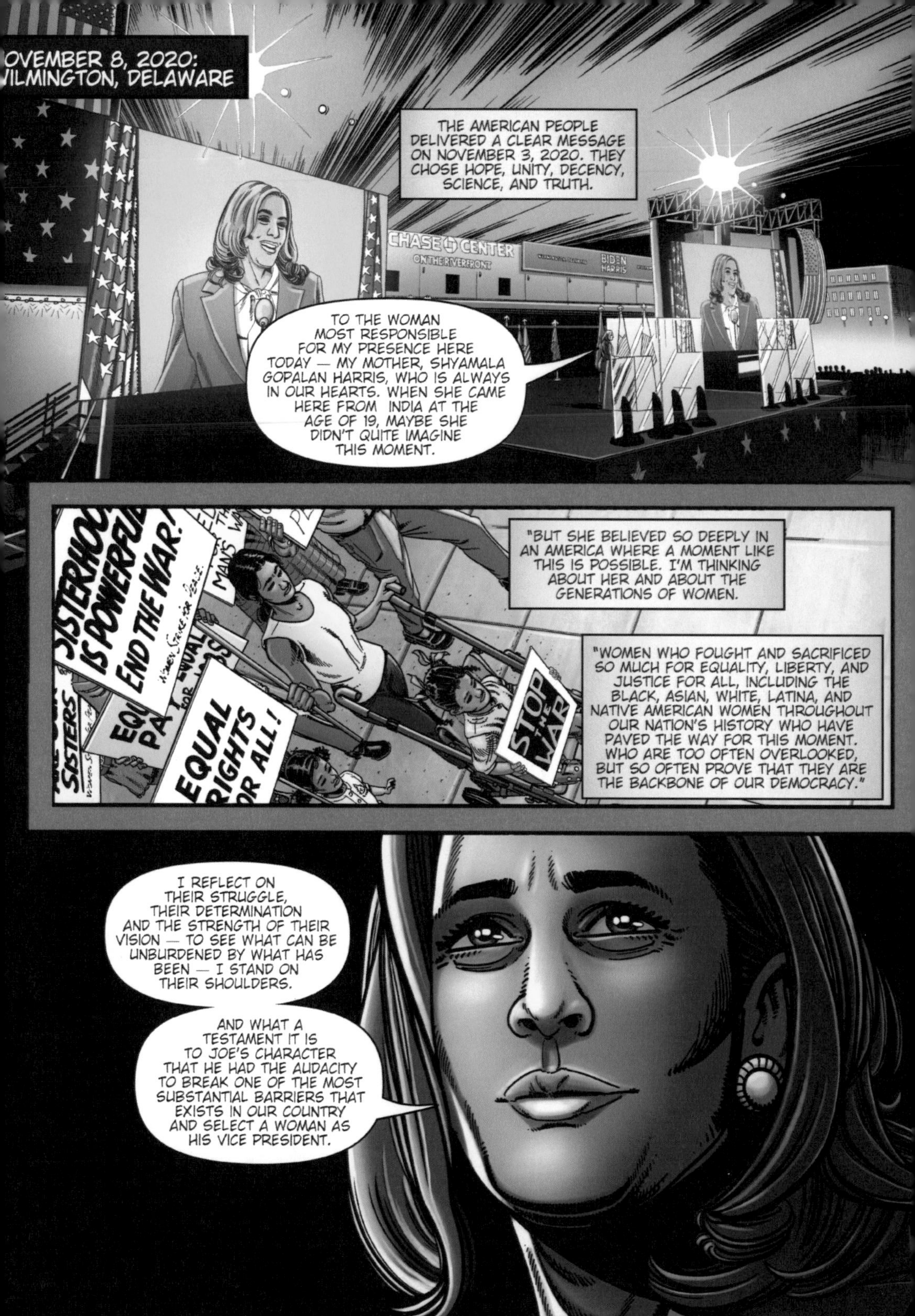
OVEMBER 8, 2020: VILMINGTON, DELAWARE
THE AMERICAN PEOPLE DELIVERED A CLEAR MESSAGE ON NOVEMBER 3, 2020. THEY CHOSE HOPE, UNITY, DECENCY, SCIENCE, AND TRUTH.
CHASE CENTER ON THE RIVERFRONT
BIDEN HARRIS
TO THE WOMAN MOST RESPONSIBLE FOR MY PRESENCE HERE TODAY — MY MOTHER, SHYAMALA GOPALAN HARRIS, WHO IS ALWAYS IN OUR HEARTS. WHEN SHE CAME HERE FROM INDIA AT THE AGE OF 19, MAYBE SHE DIDN'T QUITE IMAGINE THIS MOMENT.
"BUT SHE BELIEVED SO DEEPLY IN AN AMERICA WHERE A MOMENT LIKE THIS IS POSSIBLE. I'M THINKING ABOUT HER AND ABOUT THE GENERATIONS OF WOMEN.
END THE WAR!
STOP THE WAR
"WOMEN WHO FOUGHT AND SACRIFICED SO MUCH FOR EQUALITY, LIBERTY, AND JUSTICE FOR ALL, INCLUDING THE BLACK, ASIAN, WHITE, LATINA, AND NATIVE AMERICAN WOMEN THROUGHOUT OUR NATION'S HISTORY WHO HAVE PAVED THE WAY FOR THIS MOMENT. WHO ARE TOO OFTEN OVERLOOKED, BUT SO OFTEN PROVE THAT THEY ARE THE BACKBONE OF OUR DEMOCRACY."
I REFLECT ON THEIR STRUGGLE, THEIR DETERMINATION AND THE STRENGTH OF THEIR VISION — TO SEE WHAT CAN BE UNBURDENED BY WHAT HAS BEEN — I STAND ON THEIR SHOULDERS.
AND WHAT A TESTAMENT IT IS TO JOE'S CHARACTER THAT HE HAD THE AUDACITY TO BREAK ONE OF THE MOST SUBSTANTIAL BARRIERS THAT EXISTS IN OUR COUNTRY AND SELECT A WOMAN AS HIS VICE PRESIDENT.

"WHILE I MAY BE THE FIRST WOMAN IN THIS OFFICE, I WON'T BE THE LAST. BECAUSE EVERY LITTLE GIRL WATCHING TONIGHT SEES THAT THIS IS A COUNTRY OF POSSIBILITIES." – KAMALA HARRIS

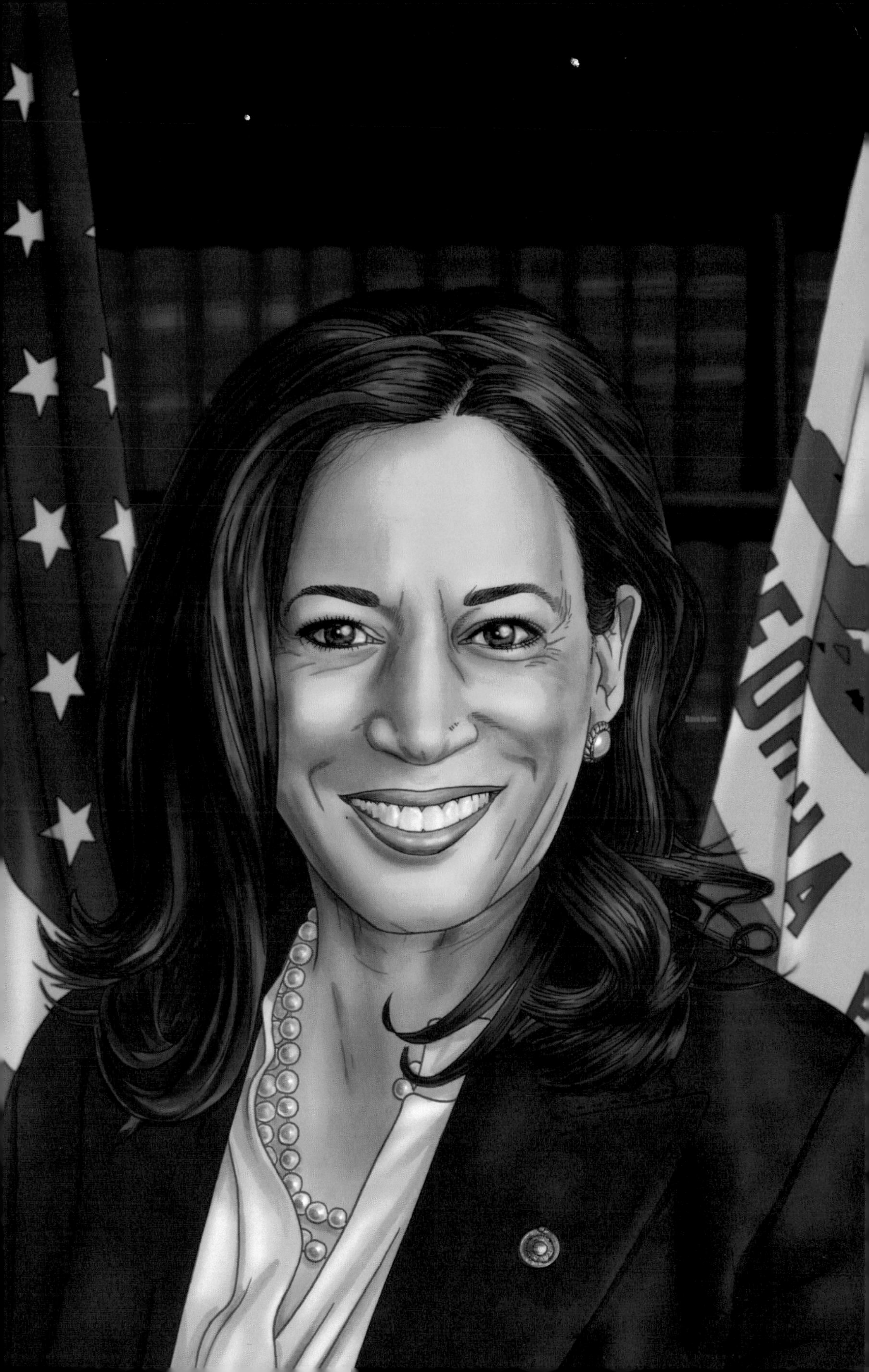

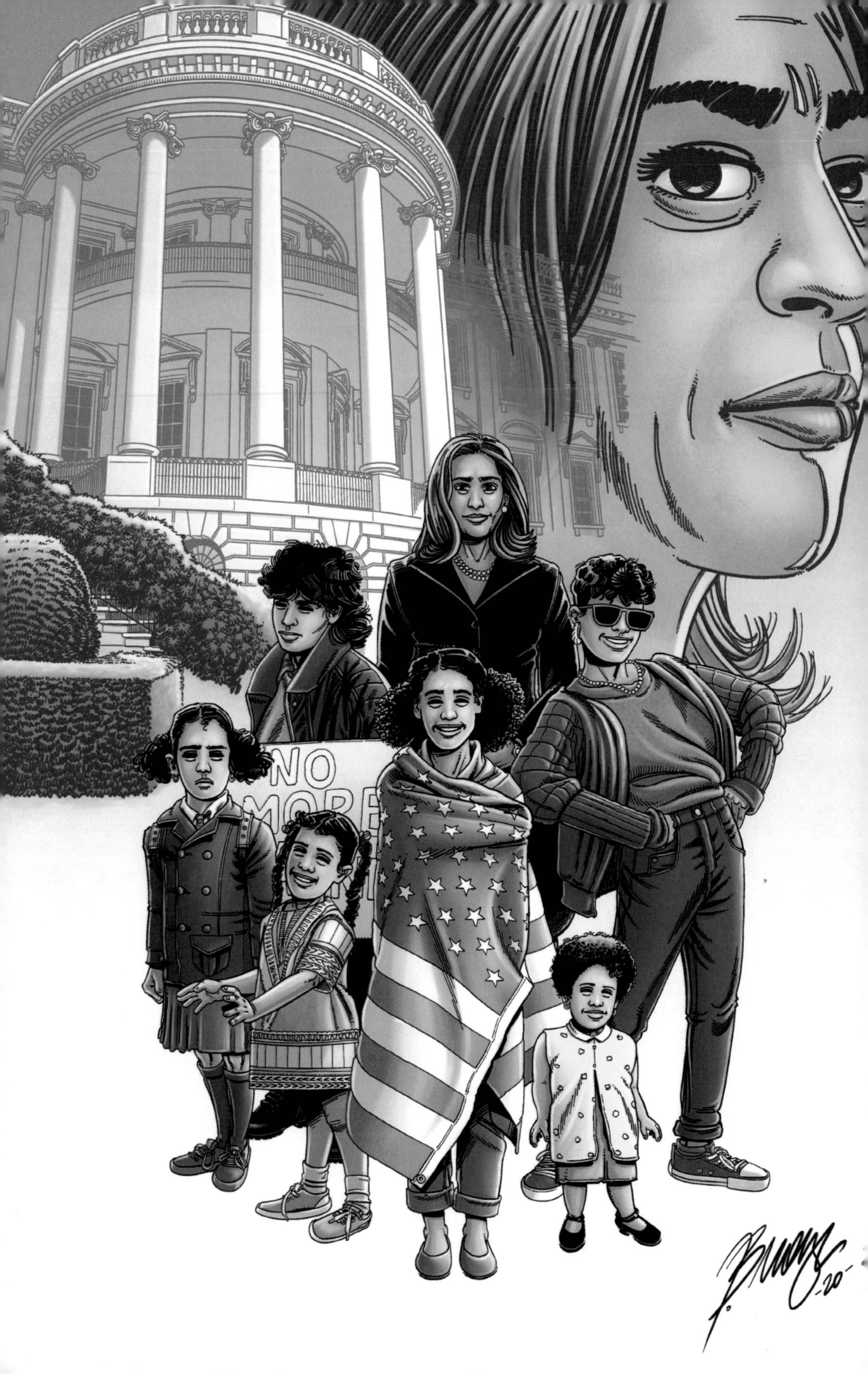
NO

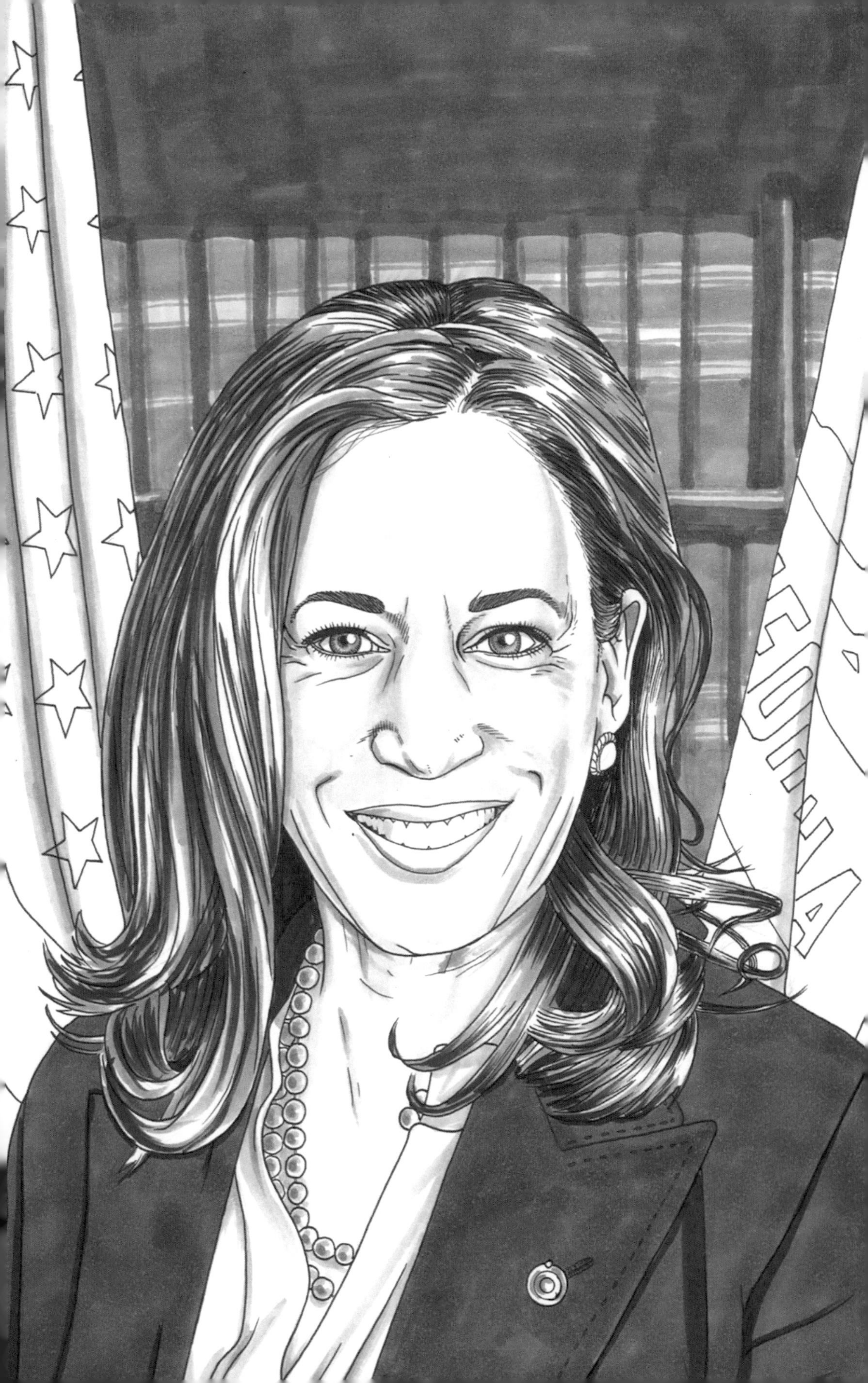

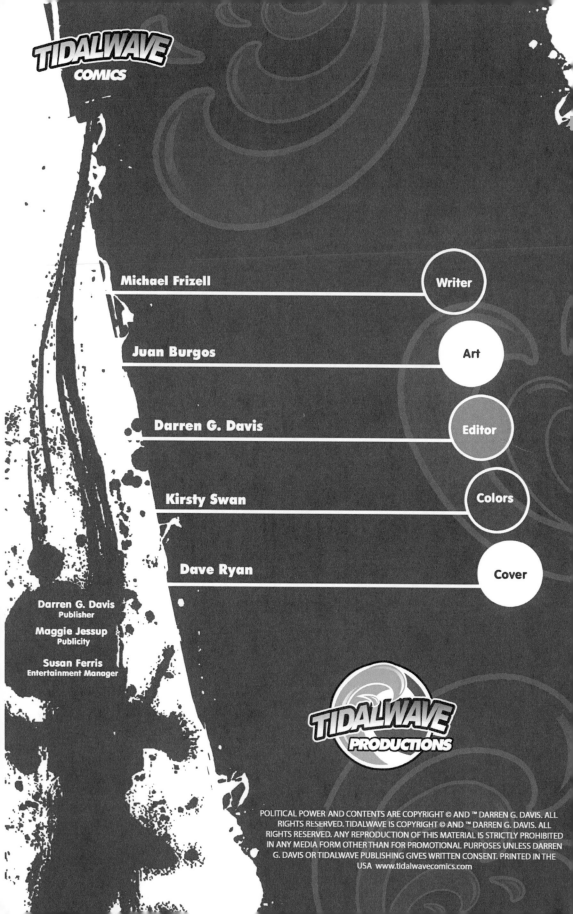

TIDALWAVE COMICS

Michael Frizell — Writer

Juan Burgos — Art

Darren G. Davis — Editor

Kirsty Swan — Colors

Dave Ryan — Cover

Darren G. Davis
Publisher

Maggie Jessup
Publicity

Susan Ferris
Entertainment Manager

TIDALWAVE PRODUCTIONS

CPSIA information can be obtained
at www.ICGtesting.com
Printed in the USA
LVRC060857280321
682727LV00009B/110